DEC 0 1 09	DATE DUE		

American Government in Action

The Presidency
of the
United States

Karen Judson

Enslow Publishers, Inc.
40 Industrial Road   PO Box 38
Box 398   Aldershot
Berkeley Heights, NJ 07922   Hants GU12 6BP
USA   UK
http://www.enslow.com

Copyright ©1996 by Karen Judson

Library of Congress Cataloging-in-Publication Data

Judson, Karen, 1941–
    The presidency of the United States / Karen Judson.
       p. cm. — (American government in action)
    Includes bibliographical references and index.
    Summary: Discusses the history, powers, and duties of the executive branch
of the United States government including the President, Vice President, the
Cabinet, and independent agencies
and commissions.
    ISBN 0-89490-585-6
    1. Presidents—United States—Juvenile literature. 2. United
States—Politics and government—Juvenile literature. [1. Presidents.] I. Title.
II. Series.
JK517.J83 1995
353.03'13—dc20
                                           95-13476
                                           CIP
                                           AC

Printed in the U.S.A.

10 9 8 7 6 5 4

Illustration Credits:
David Baldez, the White House, courtesy of the Bush Presidential
Materials Project, p. 49; Dwight D. Eisenhower Library, pp. 28, 45, 63;
Federal Bureau of Investigation, p. 12; Franklin Delano Roosevelt
Library, p. 24; Gerald R. Ford Library, p. 65; Jimmy Carter Library, p.
75; Lyndon B. Johnson Library, photo by Y.R. Okamoto, p. 80; National
Aeronautics and Space Administration (NASA), p. 94; National
Archives, p. 32; National Park Service, pp. 11, 27, 89; Press Office of
the Vice President, p. 79; Robert Knudson, White House photographer,
courtesy of the John Fitzgerald Kennedy Library, p. 34; Ronald Reagan
Library, pp. 43, 51; United States Postal Service, p. 98; the White
House, p. 104.

Cover Illustration:
© White House Historical Association; photograph by National
Geographic Society

Contents

"To the Best of My Ability"

At sunrise on the morning of April 30, 1789, thirteen guns fired a salute across Manhattan. Later that day, George Washington would be inaugurated as the first President of the United States. The ceremony would take place in Federal Hall, in New York City, the temporary site of the United States government.

President-elect Washington donned his best brown suit for his inauguration. His breeches buckled at the knee, and there were also silver buckles on his shoes. He wore a ruffled white shirt, and his long suit coat was trimmed with gold spread-eagle buttons. A dress sword encased in a leather scabbard completed the ensemble.

At the age of fifty-seven, George Washington was

an imposing figure. He stood 6 feet 3 inches tall, and weighed 200 pounds. His hands and feet were large (he wore size thirteen shoes), but he moved with athletic grace.

At 12:30 P.M. on Inauguration Day, a horse-drawn coach called for the Washingtons at their house. (George and Martha Washington had recently left Mount Vernon, their estate in Virginia, to live in New York City.) Together they rode to Federal Hall. Inside, Washington was greeted in the Senate Chamber by senators, members of the House of Representatives, and Vice President–elect John Adams.

When Washington was ready, Robert R. Livingston, chancellor of the state of New York, administered the Oath of Office, as required by the United States Constitution: "I do solemnly swear that I will faithfully execute the office of President of the United States, and will to the best of my ability, preserve, protect, and defend the Constitution of the United States."

The people who had gathered in the streets outside Federal Hall cheered as Washington began his inaugural address. "I was summoned by my country, whose voice I can never hear but with veneration and love," he told the crowd.[1]

Observers later described President Washington as dignified but nervous on his inauguration day. Thanks to a youthful habit of cracking walnuts with his jaws, Washington wore a set of false teeth carved from hippopotamus tusk.[2] The ill-fitting teeth made it difficult for him to smile, earning him a reputation among strangers as a humorless and aloof man.

Those who knew him, however, said that Washington was stately and well mannered, but that he also had a lighter side. Friends claimed he liked to flirt with the ladies, danced well, played cards and raced horses, and enjoyed fox hunting and the theater.

As the victorious commander in chief of the Continental Army during the American Revolution against Great Britain, George Washington was widely admired. After the war, however, he quickly squelched suggestions by his followers that he declare himself king of America. In fact, he was reluctant to accept the office of President. After his inauguration he said to friends, "I greatly fear that my countrymen will expect too much of me."[3]

▶ Presidential Variety

From George Washington to the present, each President of the United States has brought to the office his own unique personality traits, skills, qualifications, and goals.

The nation's highest office has been filled by wealthy men and poor men, by robust men and frail men, by self-educated men, and by graduates of Harvard, Princeton, and Yale Universities, and of the military academies of West Point and Annapolis. Several U.S. Presidents were attorneys when they began their political careers. Other occupations represented have included tailor, clothing store merchant, college professor, police commissioner, judge, newspaper publisher, mining engineer, and actor.

Some Presidents were known for their wit and humor (Abraham Lincoln, for example). Others were considered vain and cranky (John Adams). Presidential nicknames often revealed such personal traits: Old Hickory (Andrew Jackson), Old Rough and Ready (Zachary Taylor), Honest Abe (Abraham Lincoln), Silent Cal (Calvin Coolidge), The Plodder (James K. Polk), White House Iceberg (Benjamin Harrison), His Obstinacy (Grover Cleveland), and Mr. Nice Guy (Gerald Ford).

Other presidential nicknames reflected accomplishment or ability: Father of His Country (George Washington), Father of the Constitution (James Madison), Hero of Appomattox (Ulysses S. Grant), and The Great Emancipator (Abraham Lincoln). Martin Van Buren was called The Magician, for his political skill. Ronald Reagan was known as The Great Communicator for his poised public appearances.

America's Presidents have come from nineteen states. Massachusetts, New York, Ohio, and Virginia have produced many of the nation's chief executives. The following states have also seen native sons elected to the presidency: Arkansas, California, Georgia, Illinois, Iowa, Kentucky, Missouri, Nebraska, New Hampshire, New Jersey, North and South Carolina, Pennsylvania, Texas, and Vermont.

Fourteen Presidents were elected to more than one term. Presidents who served two consecutive terms (two terms in a row) include George Washington, Thomas Jefferson, James Madison, James Monroe, Andrew Jackson, Ulysses S. Grant, Theodore Roosevelt, Woodrow Wilson, Harry Truman, Dwight D. Eisenhower, and Ronald Reagan.

Grover Cleveland was the only President to serve two nonconsecutive terms. He was both the twenty-second and the twenty-fourth President. Franklin D. Roosevelt was elected to four terms, before the Twenty-second Amendment to the Constitution was passed. (This amendment limited the President to two terms in office.) Richard Nixon was reelected in 1972, but he resigned in 1974 during his second term, after the Watergate scandal.

Fourteen of the nation's Presidents served first as Vice President. The fourteen include John Adams, Thomas Jefferson, Martin Van Buren, John Tyler, Millard Fillmore, Andrew Johnson, Chester A. Arthur, Theodore Roosevelt, Calvin Coolidge, Harry Truman, Richard Nixon, Lyndon B. Johnson, Gerald Ford, and George Bush.

Eight Presidents have died in office. By odd coincidence, the Presidents elected in 1840, 1860, 1880, 1900, 1920, 1940, and 1960 all died in office. William Henry Harrison was the first President to die in office, in 1841. Harrison caught a cold after delivering his two-hour inaugural address outdoors in freezing weather. He died of pneumonia one month later.

Zachary Taylor, the twelfth President, was the second to die in office. In 1850, just one year after his inauguration, Taylor took part in Fourth of July ceremonies at the Washington Monument. Later that day he fell ill, and he died five days later. Today historians suspect that the cause of President Taylor's death was gastroenteritis—a severe, flulike irritation of the stomach and intestines.

Warren G. Harding suffered a fatal heart attack in August of 1923.

Franklin D. Roosevelt died of a cerebral hemorrhage on April 12, 1945, shortly after he was reelected to his fourth consecutive term.

Presidents Abraham Lincoln, James Garfield, William McKinley, and John F. Kennedy were assassinated while in office.

▶ The President and the Executive Branch

The President and Vice President head the executive branch of the United States government. As chief executive, the President has been given certain formal powers by the Constitution. Other powers are implied but not specifically granted by the Constitution. The President also derives authority from laws passed by Congress.

The executive branch of the federal government administers the laws passed by the legislative branch (Congress). The judicial branch (Supreme Court) interprets the laws.

Today's executive branch is made up of a large network of agencies. Each agency is directly or indirectly responsible to the President. The executive branch includes fourteen cabinet-level departments, as well as more than sixty major independent

Presidents George Washington, Thomas Jefferson, Theodore Roosevelt, and Abraham Lincoln are immortalized in stone at the Mount Rushmore Memorial in the Black Hills, near Keystone, South Dakota.

executive agencies, and at least two hundred and fifty commissions or special committees.[4]

There are approximately five hundred executive branch office buildings in Washington, D.C., alone, and many more throughout the United States and in foreign countries. (Included are all U.S. military installations, embassies and consulates, Social Security offices, and post offices.)[5] In contrast to the early days of the office, when executive branch employees could be counted in hundreds, today the executive branch employs just over three million people, excluding military personnel.[6]

Since George Washington's inauguration more than two hundred years ago, the job of President of the United States has become more demanding. The President has also become more powerful—both at home and abroad. Today, the actions of a President can and do affect every citizen of the United States, and sometimes citizens of other nations, as well.

The J. Edgar Hoover building, headquarters for the FBI, is one of the more than five hundred executive branch buildings located in Washington, D.C.

The Constitution and the Executive Branch

The European immigrants who settled in the British colonies in the 1700s were largely farmers, merchants, and laborers. In America they found a sparsely populated wilderness where land and opportunities were plentiful.

▶ Forerunners to a Federal Government

Many of the first American settlers were British subjects, who felt they were not fairly represented in England's Parliament. As colonists, they especially resented laws like the Stamp Act of 1765, which levied the first direct tax by Great Britain on the American colonies. It called for a tax to be paid on many papers and documents produced in America, including newspapers. Special stamps were to be placed on the documents, as proof that the tax had been paid.

In 1765, delegates from nine colonies (the Stamp Act Congress) met in New York to protest, among other things, "taxation without representation." The colonists petitioned England's King George III to repeal the Stamp Act, which he did in 1766.

Satisfaction over the repeal of the Stamp Act did not last. The British government had not solved its money problems, and it soon levied new taxes on the Colonies. Taxes on paint, paper, glass, lead, and tea were imposed, resulting in a new wave of political action by the American colonists.[1]

In 1774, delegates to the first Continental Congress met in Philadelphia, Pennsylvania. The delegates came from each of the thirteen colonies—Connecticut, Delaware, Georgia, Maryland, Massachusetts, New Hampshire, New Jersey, New York, North and South Carolina, Pennsylvania, Rhode Island, and Virginia. At this first session of Congress, resolutions were passed calling for a boycott against British trade.

The Continental Congress met again in 1775 to organize for war against Great Britain. The delegates appointed George Washington commander in chief of the Continental Army, to lead volunteers fighting against Great Britain in the American Revolution.

The Continental Congress reconvened in June 1776, after the beginning of the American Revolution. At this session, Virginia delegate Richard Henry Lee presented a resolution "that these United Colonies are, and of right ought to be, free and independent States." A committee was appointed to "prepare a declaration to the effect of the said first resolution."[2] The resulting Declaration of Independence was adopted on July 4, 1776.

The Articles of Confederation, written by the Continental Congress in 1777 and put into effect in 1781, provided loose guidelines for a colonial government. The Articles established a league of the thirteen colonies. They also continued Congress, now called the Congress of the Confederation, but they failed to set up a strong central government.

The American Revolution ended in 1781 with the defeat of the British by the American colonists. The 1783 Treaty of Paris officially ended the war and formally recognized American independence.

▶ Creating a Constitution

For many reasons, the Articles of Confederation proved too weak to govern the Colonies after the American Revolution. First, they failed to provide for a national chief executive who would be strong enough to administer laws and to balance legislative authority.

Another weak point was that the national government created by the Articles was entirely dependent upon the states for power and funds. The national government had no authority to regulate trade between the states, deal with other nations, or levy taxes. In fact, some states had signed treaties with other states and with the Native American tribes, bypassing the federal government.

Several problems within the Colonies also made a stronger federal government necessary. Spain was keeping American settlers out of the east bank of the Mississippi River, and Great Britain had ignored some of the provisions of the 1783 Treaty of Paris. Another major problem was the debt caused by the American Revolution. The national government had no authority to force the states to pay their share of the war debt. Some of the states that did pay used paper money backed by silver or gold, but other states printed useless paper money that was not backed by anything of value.

Taxation policies that differed from state to state also caused problems. Some states barely taxed their citizens at all, while others taxed too heavily. In those states that collected high taxes, farmers were especially hard hit. In January of 1787 eleven hundred farmers rebelled in Massachusetts. Many of the farmers were veterans of the American Revolution. They were angered by the state's refusal to issue paper money that would let them pay off their debts. The farmers took up arms against the courts, to keep them from issuing judgments for bad debts. Led by Daniel Shays, formerly a captain in the Revolutionary Army, Shays' Rebellion lasted for nearly five months. The state militia finally defeated the farmers, with no help from the weak national government. (Under the Articles of Confederation, the national government could not keep a standing peacetime army.)

Seventeen days after Shays' Rebellion ended, the states agreed to hold a convention to write a national Constitution, providing for a stronger federal government. The fifty-five delegates opened the Constitutional Convention in Philadelphia in May 1787. By September, the seven Articles of the Constitution had been hammered out, and were submitted to all thirteen states for ratification. Approval by nine states was needed for the Constitution to take effect, and the ninth state—New Hampshire—ratified in June 1788. The Constitution went into effect on the first Wednesday in March 1789. The last of the thirteen states—Rhode Island—ratified the Constitution in 1790.

The Constitution was approved by most states with the condition that a list of individual liberties, guaranteed by the new government, would be added in the form of a Bill of Rights. Therefore, one of the first acts of the first Congress of the United States when it met in 1789 was to begin working on a Bill of Rights.

▶ A Balance of Power

The United States Constitution established the three branches of government that exist today. The legislative branch, consisting of a Congress made up of a Senate and a House of Representatives, makes laws and raises money to finance the government. The executive branch, headed by the President and Vice President, administers the laws. The judicial branch, led by nine Justices appointed to the Supreme Court, interprets the laws. The judicial branch also acts as a mediator (peacemaker) between the three branches of government, and between the government and the people.

Several constitutional provisions grant specific authority to each branch of the government. These provisions provide the checks and balances that keep any one branch from grabbing too much power. Congress creates laws, and can change them at any time. Laws written by Congress can be vetoed by the President. They can also be ruled unconstitutional by the Supreme Court. When the President vetoes a bill, his veto can be overruled only by a two-thirds vote by both the Senate and the House of Representatives.

▶ Congressional Power

Congress can create and destroy agencies of the federal government, and determines whether an agency will be located within the executive branch. Congress can define exactly what an agency has the power to do, and can make that agency completely independent of the President. Congress also has the power of appropriation (funding), which allows it to exercise power by controlling the available money. This means that unless Congress votes to fund an agency, that agency cannot exist.

Congress may delegate authority to the executive branch by allowing the President and executive departments to define laws and programs, and to decide how they are to be put into effect.

▶ Presidential Power

Presidential power refers to a President's authority, as given to him by:

- the laws passed by Congress

- precedents (established practices) set by each former President
- constitutional directives

The President has two kinds of power. The first is formal power, which is spelled out in the Constitution, in laws passed by Congress, and in judicial rulings. The second is inherent power, which comes from on-the-job interpretation of the laws as applied to each situation a President may face while in office.[3]

Pardoning convicted criminals is an example of a formal power of the President, because it is specifically mentioned in the Constitution. The power to seize private property during wartime is an example of an inherent power. The Constitution does not state specifically that the President may do this, yet it has been done in time of war. (See "Emergency Powers" in chapter 3.)

Inherent powers stem from two statements in Article II of the Constitution: Section 1—"the executive power shall be vested in a President of the United States of America"; and Section 3—the President "shall take care that the laws be faithfully executed." The wording of these two sections gives the President wide leeway for acting during times of emergency.

Presidential power also refers to the influence the President has over foreign affairs, governmental operations, and public opinion.

As head of the executive branch, the President supervises many government departments and agencies, and administers the laws and programs created by Congress. He also introduces legislation, and appoints people to government office, although many of the President's appointments are subject to approval by Congress. The President needs authority from Congress for starting and funding new programs.

The President is subject to the same laws as any other citizen, and is accountable to the Supreme Court. He can be impeached (removed from office) by Congress for certain offenses.

▶ Judicial Power

The Supreme Court interprets the Constitution. The nine Supreme Court Justices decide whether or not decisions made by lower courts and laws passed by Congress are constitutional. The President appoints the Court's Justices, with approval of the Senate. Congress appropriates funds for the Court's operation.

▶ Constitutional Mandates

Powers of the three branches of the government derive from the seven Articles of the Constitution. Article I gives legislative powers to Congress. In Sections 1 through 10, the composition, qualifications, and duties of members of the House of Representatives and the Senate are established. General powers of Congress are covered here, including: borrowing money, regulating commerce, levying and collecting taxes, declaring war, organizing the military, passing laws necessary to enforce the Constitution, and other important matters of state.

In Article II, four sections cover the President and his power as chief executive. (See "Presidential Power" above.)

Article II, Section 1 of the Constitution also creates the office of Vice President, and says both the President and Vice President will serve four-year terms of office.

In addition, Section 1 says the President will be paid for serving, and the executive salary cannot be changed during the President's term of office. This section also contains the President's Oath of Office.

Further sections in Article II cover the presidential functions of making treaties, appointing ambassadors, filling vacancies in office during Senate recess, giving advice to Congress, and impeaching civil officers.

Because the Constitution is vague in defining specific powers and limits of the presidency, some Presidents have expanded their authority through individual interpretation. In his own words, Thomas Jefferson "stretched the Constitution till it cracked," when he used his presidential treaty-making powers to buy the Louisiana Territory from Napoleon in 1803.[4] Theodore Roosevelt believed that the President should take whatever action was necessary for the public good, as long as it was not expressly forbidden by law or the Constitution. "I did not usurp power," he wrote of his presidency, "but I did greatly broaden the use of executive power."[5]

Theodore Roosevelt's view of the use of presidential power contrasted strongly with that of Whig Presidents William Henry Harrison, John Tyler, Zachary Taylor, and Millard Fillmore. These Presidents stuck strictly to the limits of the Constitution and left legislative duties to Congress, in agreement with the Whig Party platform.[6] (The Whig Party merged with the new Republican Party in the 1850s.)

▶ Executive Privilege

Executive privilege is an idea taken from the constitutional principle of separation of powers. Claiming executive privilege allows the President to withhold information from Congress, the courts, and the public. The practice began years ago, at a time when the President's few close personal assistants needed protection from a prying Congress. Under current practice, only the President may formally invoke executive privilege, either on his own behalf or on behalf of other officials within the executive branch.

In one of the most widely reported examples of the use of executive privilege, in 1974 President Richard Nixon tried to withhold taped recordings of the Watergate conversations by claiming executive privilege. The Supreme Court ruled that the protection did not apply, and ordered President Nixon to obey a subpoena (court-issued demand) for the tapes.[7]

▶ Choosing a President

Presidents and Vice Presidents are the only government officials elected by the entire nation. In theory, as stated in Article II, Section 1 of the Constitution, anyone can be elected President who is:

1. a natural-born citizen of the United States;

2. at least thirty-five years of age; and

3. a resident of the United States for a minimum of fourteen years.

Six constitutional amendments affect elections, voters, or terms in office for the President and Vice President:

The Twelfth Amendment, passed in 1804, changed the way electors voted for the President and Vice President. Under this amendment, electors would cast separate ballots for the President and the Vice President, instead of voting for them on the same ballot, as they had in the past. (See "Electoral College" below.)

The Nineteenth Amendment, passed in 1920, gave women the right to vote.

The Twentieth ("Lame Duck") Amendment, passed in 1932, said that the terms of the outgoing President and Vice President would end at noon on the 20th day of January. (*Lame duck* is the term used to describe public officials who are serving out remaining days in office after having been defeated for reelection, or when not seeking reelection.)

The Twenty-second Amendment, ratified in 1951, limited a President to two elected terms, or a total of ten years in office, if the President succeeded to the position before being elected. A President can succeed to the position without being elected if, for instance, the President in office dies, resigns, or cannot serve for some other reason. The Vice President would then become President, and would be limited to a total of ten years in office.

The Twenty-third Amendment, passed in 1961, granted presidential election voting rights to residents of the District of Columbia. It also gave Washington, D.C., three electors.

The Twenty-sixth Amendment, passed in 1971, gave eighteen-year-olds the right to vote. Previously, voters had to be twenty-one.

President Franklin D. Roosevelt and First Lady Eleanor, riding in their third inaugural parade on January 20, 1941. When Roosevelt died in office in 1945, Vice President Harry Truman became President.

▶ The Electoral College

Article II, Section 1 of the Constitution provides for the selection of the President and Vice President. Presidential elections must be held regularly, once every four years, in years divisible by the number four. The election process must originate in states, acting through duly chosen representatives called electors.

The framers of the Constitution decided not to let Congress choose the President, because they wanted the people to have a vote. However, Constitutional Convention delegates from the Southern states would not agree to a popular vote for the presidency, because slaves could not vote. Since northern states would have more registered voters, the southern states could be at a disadvantage in electing a candidate sympathetic to their interests. The electoral college system for electing a President and Vice President was created as a compromise. Under the electoral college system, voters in a presidential election actually vote for electors—persons expected to support a specific candidate.

A state is assigned as many electors as it has senators and representatives in Congress. No state has fewer than three electoral votes. (The District of Columbia gets three, even though it has no members in Congress.) Each state's electors are chosen early in a presidential-election year, either by popular vote or by the state legislature, depending upon state law. The Constitution states that senators, representatives, and other persons "holding an office of trust or profit under the United States" cannot serve as electors.

When the electors meet in their state capitals in December of a presidential-election year, they cast two votes, on two separate ballots. One vote is cast for President, and one for Vice President. The electors are pledged to the candidates chosen by their national political party conventions. To be elected, presidential candidates must have a majority of the electoral votes—currently 270 out of 538.

In three presidential elections, the candidate with the largest popular vote failed to win a majority of electoral votes:

- In 1824, when none of the four candidates for President received a majority of the electoral college votes, the House of Representatives chose John Quincy Adams.
- In 1876, Samuel J. Tilden won a majority of the popular vote, but he lost the presidency to Rutherford B. Hayes by one electoral vote.
- In 1888, Benjamin Harrison received 100,000 fewer popular votes than Grover Cleveland, but won the electoral vote 233 to 168.

Originally, electors were required to cast a single ballot with the names of two candidates on it. The electors did not specify which name would be President, and which Vice President. After the ballots were counted, the candidate with the most votes (if the total was a majority of all votes cast) was elected President. The candidate who came in second became Vice President.

This procedure was changed by constitutional amendment after the election of 1800. That year, electors from the Democratic-Republican party named both a President and a Vice President from their own party. ("Republican" was later dropped from the party's name.) The result was a tie between Thomas Jefferson and Aaron Burr. The House of Representatives then voted for the President, as provided for in the Constitution in the case of a tie. After thirty-five deadlocked ballots, Thomas Jefferson was finally elected President.

The Twelfth Amendment to the Constitution, ratified before the next presidential election in 1804, changed the procedure. The amendment allowed electors to vote separately for President and Vice President. The effect of this change was that a tie was not as likely to occur as before.

Harry Truman waves at the beginning of his 1948 campaign tour. The Presidential Seal is visible, on the back of the train. (President Truman changed the position of the eagle so it faced the viewer's left.)

The electoral college method for choosing presidential candidates made electors agents of political party will. In later elections (including today's elections), candidates needed the party nomination in order to be on the ballot for President. The vote of the electoral college is now largely a formality. There have been many unsuccessful attempts to abolish the electoral college system.

▶ Nominating a Candidate for President

The Constitution makes no provision for choosing the candidates for President and Vice President. From 1796 until 1824, all the leading candidates for President were nominated by congressional caucus, because no one seemed to know a better way to do it. (A caucus is a closed meeting of a select group, held to choose candidates or decide policy.) The

President Dwight D. Eisenhower and First Lady Mamie Eisenhower campaign for re-election in November, 1956. "Whistle Stop" campaigns were popular for many years.

congressional caucus met for the last time as a nominating body in the 1824 election. After that, other groups, such as state legislatures and political meetings, nominated the candidates for President and Vice President.

By the 1830s, all candidates for President and Vice President were nominated by national political party conventions. This practice continues today.

▶ When the President Is Unable to Serve

Article II, Section 1 of the Constitution also provides for filling the office of President, in case an elected President dies, becomes incapacitated (disabled) while in office, resigns, or for any other reason cannot serve out the term.

The Vice President is first in line to take over the presidency, if the President is unable to carry out his duties. Next in line for President, if the Vice President cannot serve, is the speaker of the House of Representatives. Then comes the president pro tempore (Latin, meaning "for the time being") of the Senate. If none of these officials can serve as President, the Cabinet Department heads are chosen, in the following order: secretary of State; secretary of the Treasury; secretary of Defense; attorney general; secretary of the Interior; secretary of Agriculture; secretary of Commerce; secretary of Labor; secretary of Health and Human Services; secretary of Housing and Urban Development; secretary of Transportation; secretary of Energy; secretary of Education; and the secretary of Veterans' Affairs.

The person appointed to serve out a President's unfinished term serves only until a new President is chosen in a regular presidential election.

▶ Removal by Impeachment

Article II, Section 4 of the Constitution states: "The President, Vice President, and all civil officers of the United States shall be removed from office on impeachment for, and conviction of, treason, bribery, or other high crimes and misdemeanors."

Under Article I of the Constitution, the House of Representatives has the sole power of impeachment, and the Senate has the sole power to try all impeachments. In other words, the decision to impeach (charge with an offense) is made by a vote in the House of Representatives. If the vote is "yes," the Senate tries the case. The Chief Justice of the Supreme Court presides over the trial. A conviction requires a two-thirds vote of Senate members present.

In the history of the presidency, only one President has been impeached. Vice President Andrew Johnson became President in 1865 after Abraham Lincoln's assassination. Johnson was a Democrat who favored states' rights, and he opposed most of the Civil War Reconstruction Acts passed by the Republican Congress. Over Johnson's veto, Congress passed the Tenure of Office Act, which forbade the President to remove from office any federal official who had been appointed with the advice and consent of the Senate. Sure that the Tenure of Office Act was unconstitutional, President

Johnson dismissed Secretary of War Edwin M. Stanton.

For his violation of the Tenure of Office Act, in 1868 the House of Representatives voted eleven counts of impeachment against President Johnson, including failure to take care that the laws are faithfully executed. Johnson was tried by the Senate and acquitted (cleared of the charges) by one vote. The Tenure of Office Act was repealed in 1887.

A second President resigned under the threat of impeachment. Richard Nixon, a Republican, was elected to his second term as President in November 1972. In June of 1972, five employees of the Committee to Reelect the President, Nixon's personal campaign organization, were caught breaking into Democratic National Committee headquarters in the Watergate complex in Washington, D.C. The men broke into the building to repair electronic listening devices that earlier had been secretly installed.

An investigation uncovered the involvement of a number of high-level administration officials in attempts to cover up the break-in. Two former cabinet officers and twenty-six other members of Nixon's administration were charged with various crimes. Some were convicted and served prison terms. President Nixon denied having had any personal involvement. The courts forced him to turn over tape recordings indicating that he had known about criminal activity by his staff members and that he had tried to divert the investigation.[8]

Impeachment seemed certain, and President

President Richard Nixon (right) and Vice President Spiro Agnew at Camp David, on August 15, 1972. Nixon was the only President to resign the office. Agnew resigned as well, after an investigation for failure to pay income taxes.

Nixon resigned on August 9, 1974. Vice President Gerald Ford became President. One month later President Ford made the surprise announcement that he had granted Nixon a "full, free, and absolute pardon for all offenses" committed during his administration.[9] Some congressional leaders called the pardon a "misuse of power," and questions were raised about its constitutionality. In defending his action, Ford stated: "I am absolutely convinced, when dealing with the reality in this very, very difficult situation that I made the right decision in an effort, an honest conscientious effort, to end the discussions and turmoil in the United States."[10]

Roles of the President

In October of 1962 the world teetered on the brink of nuclear war. The Soviet Union had placed intercontinental ballistic missiles in Cuba and had aimed them at the United States. President John F. Kennedy demanded that Soviet Premier Nikita Khrushchev remove the missiles, or risk military action by the United States. Thirteen days after receiving the U.S. ultimatum, Premier Khrushchev ordered removal of the missiles. People around the world sighed with relief. At the height of the crisis President Kennedy remarked, "I guess this is the week I earn my salary."[1]

The President earns his salary by assuming many roles. When categorizing the President's roles, most experts refer to Clinton Rossiter's list from his book *The American Presidency*. The President fulfills his constitutional duties by serving as the nation's chief executive, chief legislator, chief diplomat, commander in chief, and chief of state. To this list Rossiter adds roles as political party chief, voice of the people, protector of the peace, and manager of prosperity (chief economist.)[2]

▶ The President as Chief Executive

As chief executive of the federal government, the President appoints and may dismiss certain officials. He also oversees the budget process and serves as chief law enforcement officer. To help the President function as chief executive, the Executive Office of the President (EOP) was created. The EOP is made up of a collection of temporary and permanent agencies. The composition of the EOP changes to meet

President John F. Kennedy (center) meets with Secretary of Defense Robert S. McNamara, and Chairman of the Joint Chiefs Maxwell Taylor in the cabinet room at the White House on January 25, 1963.

the specific needs of each President. The Executive Office of the President, the cabinet, and other executive department agencies and commissions are discussed further in chapter 5.

▶ Power of Appointment

As the size of the federal government increased, Presidents had to delegate more authority to appointed officials. Today, one of the most important powers of the President is that of finding and appointing persons to fill high-level posts in government.

The top officers of the executive branch are appointed by the President and are responsible to him. The Senate must approve most of the President's major appointments. These appointees are usually replaced when the President who selected them leaves office. (Other executive branch employees are hired under the Civil Service system, and are not automatically replaced when a President leaves office.)

▶ The Budget

The Constitution does not mention the President's role in the budget process. However, Article II, Section 3 says that the President may recommend to Congress "such measures as he shall judge necessary and expedient." Implied in this phrase is the power of the President to present a financial plan to Congress.[3]

The Budget and Accounting Act of 1921 put the President in charge of the fiscal management of the executive branch. Congress made budgeting an executive function in hopes of controlling spending within the growing executive branch.[4] This act also established the Bureau of the Budget. The Bureau of the Budget was moved from the Treasury Department to the EOP in 1939. It was renamed the Office of Management and Budget (OMB) in 1972.

Overseeing the budget process has become one of the major powers of the President. With help from the Office of Management and Budget, the President prepares a budget each year. He recommends how much money Congress should allot for each department of the government, and for various national programs. The President can delay or cancel funds set aside by Congress for a particular purpose, but this action is subject to the agreement of Congress, in accordance with the Congressional Budget and Impoundment Control Act of 1974.

▶ Law Enforcement Power

The Constitution does not specifically give the federal government the power to regulate the health, safety, morals, or general welfare of citizens, but Article I, Section 8 says Congress shall have the power "to make all laws which shall be necessary and proper for carrying into execution the foregoing powers, and all other powers vested by this Constitution in the Government of the United States, or in any Department or Officer thereof." It is this clause that gives the government, and the President as its chief executive, police and regulatory powers.

The Constitution further provides for the President's law enforcement powers in Article II, Section 3, which charges the President to "take care that the laws be faithfully executed."

In 1894, when railroad workers in Chicago violated an injunction against striking, Grover Cleveland used federal troops to enforce the injunction because the strike was interfering with delivery of the mail. To enforce federal law, in 1957 Dwight D. Eisenhower sent troops to help integrate a public school in Little Rock, Arkansas. John F. Kennedy said, "Under the Constitution I have to carry out the law," when he ordered U.S. marshals to Oxford, Mississippi, in 1962. Kennedy sent the marshals to enforce a federal court order allowing James Meredith, an African American who had previously been denied admission, to enroll at the University of Mississippi.[5]

Law enforcement agencies within the executive branch include the Federal Bureau of Investigation, the Drug Enforcement Administration, Border Patrol, U.S. Marshals Service, Secret Service, Coast Guard, Offices of Inspector General, and others. Regulatory agencies that enforce the law are discussed in chapter 6.

Article II, Section 2 of the Constitution also gives the President the power to grant reprieves and pardons "for offenses against the United States, except in cases of impeachment." A reprieve is an order to delay the punishment of a convicted and sentenced criminal. When the President grants clemency, he reduces a convicted criminal's punishment. Neither a reprieve nor clemency erases guilt. A pardon erases both sentence and guilt, as if the crime had never been committed.

The President may grant amnesty by issuing a blanket pardon to all persons who have violated a certain national law. The soldiers who fought for the Confederacy in the Civil War were granted amnesty by Presidents Abraham Lincoln and Andrew Johnson. Harry Truman signed amnesties for draft evaders after World War II, and Jimmy Carter did the same after the Vietnam War.

▶ Executive Orders

Under authority implied by the "executive power" clause of Article II, Section 1 of the Constitution, Presidents may issue executive orders. Executive orders are based on existing laws, or on the President's duties as defined in the Constitution. These directives become law without prior approval of Congress.

Executive orders are usually issued for one of three reasons: to set up administrative agencies or to change the practices of an agency, to enforce laws passed by Congress, or to make treaties with foreign powers. Sometimes executive orders affect private citizens as well as government agencies and officials. For example, Lyndon B. Johnson's Executive Order 11246 changed employment practices in the private sector. The order required firms that receive government contracts to create programs for hiring more minorities.[6]

▶ Emergency Powers

When the framers of the Constitution planned a government with many checks and balances, they built in some deadlock (situations in which no compromise could be reached). They realized, however, that there would be times, such as wartime, when the government would have to move quickly. Article II of the Constitution empowers the President to "preserve, protect, and defend" the Constitution and to uphold its provisions. This allows the President to act quickly in emergency situations, without first getting the approval of Congress.

According to Congressional Quarterly's *Powers of the Presidency*, there are three types of emergency powers the President can use:[7]

Powers over individuals. The President can order the confinement of persons believed to be threats to national security. He can also restrict the travel of Americans within the country, and to some countries abroad, for example, Cuba. He can keep foreigners out of the United States, and can require certain groups to register with the government, for example, gun owners. He can suspend writs of habeas corpus, which is the only emergency power specifically mentioned in the Constitution (Article I). (A writ of habeas corpus is a document that says a jailer must bring a prisoner to court for a judgment on whether or not imprisonment was legal.) The President can also send armed forces to fight in foreign nations and declare martial law.

Martial law replaces civilian government with

military rule. Presidents must justify a decision to declare martial law by showing that the nation's security and welfare are at stake. No President has ever placed the entire country under total martial law.

George Washington set the precedent for Presidents to declare martial law. After the Whiskey Rebellion of 1794, he ordered all rebels to be delivered to civil courts for trial. No President has declared martial law directly on behalf of the federal government since Abraham Lincoln placed some areas of the country under martial law during the Civil War.[8]

Powers over property. The President can order stockpiling of vital materials like uranium. He can place restrictions on exports such as computers. He can order rationing of materials to help with defense. He can also fix wages and prices, and he can require industries to give first choice to government contracts, in manufacturing or selling goods.

Powers over communications. The President can withhold from Congress and the public information that he considers vital to national security. He can censor communications with other nations. He can require official representatives of foreign nations to register with the U.S. government.

Presidents have used their emergency powers extensively in times of war. Abraham Lincoln claimed emergency war powers after the Civil War began. Congress was not in session when the first shots were fired at Fort Sumter on April 12, 1861, but Lincoln sent help to the fort at once. Before he convened Congress, Lincoln called out the militia, placed a blockade on Southern ports, enlarged the army and navy, and ordered the Department of Treasury to pay for his war actions.[9]

In times of emergency, Congress has made it easier for the President to use his powers. During World War I, President Woodrow Wilson succeeded in having Congress pass laws giving him certain wartime powers over the economy. During World War II, President Franklin D. Roosevelt was given the power to seize and operate more than sixty strike-threatened industries. Congress also approved Roosevelt's evacuation of 70,000 Japanese Americans from the West Coast of the United States.[10]

Presidents have also used their emergency powers during economic crises. A good example is the action of Franklin D. Roosevelt in 1933. On March 4, he declared a national state of emergency and closed the banks to keep the nation's economy from collapsing. Congress gave its approval by passing the Emergency Banking Act three days later. This law, together with the Securities Exchange Act of 1934, empowered the President to declare a state of national financial martial law.[11]

▶ The President as Chief Legislator

Under the U.S. Constitution, the legislative branch of the government (Congress) has the chief authority to make laws. The legislative powers of the President are listed in the Constitution under Article II, Section 3 and Article I, Section 7. He is to give

Congress "information of the state of the union," should recommend "such measures as he shall judge necessary and expedient," and can approve or veto bills passed by Congress.

Under current custom, the President also drafts legislation to present to Congress. When the President wants to influence the passage of legislation he favors, he may invite key Congressmen to dine (or jog) with him, promise them favors, threaten a veto, or hold a press conference to complain about a deadlocked Congress.

William H. Taft was the first modern President to draft legislation to present to Congress. (Congress reportedly resented Taft's boldness.) Woodrow Wilson, who followed Taft as President, started the practice of presenting bills to Congress in person. The press, for the first time in history, spoke of the "administration's bills" in Congress. President Warren G. Harding tried to go further when he addressed the Senate from the Vice President's chair, asking for defeat of a pending bill on soldiers' bonuses. The bill was defeated, but there was much angry debate about the President's "unconstitutional" appearance.

Franklin D. Roosevelt's presidency began a period of major legislative influence for the President that continues today. Much of the New Deal legislation was drafted by President Roosevelt's office or an agency of the executive branch. (The New Deal was a group of programs set up to improve conditions for Americans during the Great Depression.)

▶ State of the Union Message

The Constitution says that the President will, "from time to time, give to the Congress information of the state of the union." It does not say how this should be done. Presidents George Washington and John Adams delivered their State of the Union messages in speeches to Congress. Thomas Jefferson began a long tradition of Presidents giving their reports to Congress in writing. After Jefferson left office, a President did not again appear before Congress to deliver the State of the Union Address until Woodrow Wilson.[12]

The State of the Union address has become an important way for the President to inform and influence Congress and the people. Today, the address is delivered in person by the President to both houses

President Ronald Reagan (foreground) delivering a State of the Union Address. Vice President George Bush and Speaker of the House Jim Wright are seated in the background.

of Congress. It is also broadcast to a worldwide television audience.

▶ The Veto

The veto, the ability to block acts passed by Congress, is one of the President's most important legislative powers. The Constitution says that every bill passed by both houses of Congress must be approved by the President before it can become law. The President has three choices. He can sign the bill into law, veto the bill by returning it to the originating house within ten days, or do nothing. If the President does nothing, the bill automatically becomes law after ten days.

If Congress again passes a bill after the President has vetoed it (with a two-thirds majority in each house), the bill overrides the President's veto and becomes law.

A pocket veto occurs if the President does nothing, and Congress adjourns before the ten-day time limit passes.

Bills vetoed by the President are usually sent back to Congress with a message explaining the President's reasons for the veto. In this way, the President's veto allows him to make a policy statement to Congress (and also to the American public, using the media.)

The first six Presidents used the veto only for bills they considered unconstitutional. Andrew Jackson, the seventh President, was the first to veto legislation for political reasons. During Jackson's eight years in office, he used the veto twelve

President Dwight D. Eisenhower signs a highway legislation bill on May 6, 1954.

times—more than all the vetoes issued by all the Presidents before him. Presidents who came after Jackson followed his example in using the veto as a political tool.[13]

▶ The President as Chief Diplomat

As the nation's chief diplomat, the President conducts business with foreign nations. He appoints ambassadors and other diplomats to represent America in other countries. He receives ambassadors from other nations and negotiates treaties and executive agreements. He formally recognizes new governments and nations and directs the U.S. delegation to the United Nations. He also directs communications with foreign powers. The President shares diplomatic powers with Congress, but the President's foreign relations policies are usually dominant.

As chief diplomat, the President often travels to other nations to meet personally with their leaders. Theodore Roosevelt was the first President to travel outside the continental United States. Woodrow Wilson was the first American President to travel to Europe while in office. Richard Nixon was the first U.S. President to visit the former Soviet Union and the People's Republic of China.

▶ Treaties

The Constitution gives the President the power to make treaties with foreign nations, but says they must be approved by two-thirds of the Senate. If the Senate approves a treaty, it becomes law only if the President ratifies (approves) it.

▶ Executive Agreements

Presidents may also make executive agreements with other nations. Unlike treaties, executive agreements do not require Senate approval. Like treaties, executive agreements may be set aside by the legislature. Executive agreements made by one President are not binding on a future administration without the new President's consent.

In 1803, with the Louisiana Purchase, Thomas Jefferson paved the way for future Presidents to use executive agreements. Jefferson made a deal with Napoleon, the Emperor of France, to purchase the Louisiana Territory for $15 million (about three cents an acre). The Constitution makes no provision for acquiring new territory, but Jefferson was afraid Napoleon would change his mind in the time it would take to get a constitutional amendment passed, so he made the deal before sending the proposal to the Senate for approval. "The less said about any constitutional difficulty, the better," he told Congress.[14] The plan was approved by the Senate in the fall of 1803, soon after the deal was made.

▶ The President as Commander in Chief

The framers of the Constitution divided war-making powers between the legislative and executive branches of the government. They made the President the commander in chief of U.S. military forces, and gave him the power to make treaties to end war. Only Congress can declare war.

Congress has declared war just five times in U.S. history:

1. Against Great Britain in the War of 1812 (President James Madison).

2. Against Mexico in the Mexican War of 1846 (President James K. Polk).

3. Against Spain in 1898 in the Spanish-American War (President William McKinley).

4. Against Germany in 1917 (President Woodrow Wilson), marking America's entry into World War I.

5. Against Japan, Germany, and Italy in 1941 (President Franklin D. Roosevelt), during World War II.

Several Presidents have sent troops to fight in

"armed conflicts" that were not declared wars. The Civil War was never officially declared by Congress, but Abraham Lincoln used his war powers extensively. During the 1800s various Presidents authorized military action in Cuba, Greece, China, Puerto Rico, and Nicaragua—all without declarations of war. In 1950 Harry Truman sent troops to fight an undeclared war with North Korea. In the undeclared Vietnam War, 58,135 Americans died between 1964 and 1975, during Lyndon Johnson's and Richard Nixon's administrations.[15]

More recently, Jimmy Carter sent troops to rescue American hostages in Iran in 1980. (The mission failed when a U.S. military helicopter and a C-130 collided.) Ronald Reagan ordered the U.S. military to invade the Caribbean island of Grenada on October 25, 1983. In 1990, George Bush sent troops to the Persian Gulf after Iraq's dictator, Saddam Hussein, captured Kuwait. In 1994, Bill Clinton sent military forces to help restore Haiti's elected President to office. That same year, Clinton again ordered troops to Kuwait, when Iraq's Saddam Hussein moved his army into position near Kuwait's border.

▶ War Powers Resolution

The War Powers Resolution was passed by Congress in 1973, over President Richard Nixon's veto. This resolution requires the President to confer with Congress before committing troops to fight. If advance discussion is impossible, the President has to inform Congress of his actions within forty-eight hours. Then, if Congress does not declare war or consent to

President George Bush (center) eating Thanksgiving dinner with the troops in the Persian Gulf, November 22, 1990.

the action, the President has sixty to ninety days to order a withdrawal. Congress can bypass the time limitation by passing a joint resolution, which the President cannot veto. The effectiveness of the War Powers Resolution in limiting the President's war powers has been questioned.

The worldwide development of atomic weapons has raised the concern over who can "push the button" in times of crisis. In the United States, the President can decide to use nuclear weapons, without the approval or possibly even the knowledge of Congress. President Harry Truman used this option in 1945, during World War II, when he ordered the dropping of atomic bombs on Hiroshima and Nagasaki, Japan, leading to Japan's surrender.[16]

▶ The President as Chief of State

The President has always been the ceremonial head of the United States government. Today he presides over hundreds of ceremonies. He accepts a donated turkey for the White House Thanksgiving dinner; lights the nation's Christmas tree; opens the Easter egg roll on the White House lawn; shakes the hands of award-winning teachers, athletes, and heroes; and hosts state dinners for visiting diplomats.

Presidents may delegate state functions to others. First Ladies tour foreign nations. Sons and daughters of presidents give speeches at banquets. Vice Presidents attend state funerals. Cabinet secretaries visit schools and hospitals. Even close friends of the President occasionally may stand in for him.

Though the President's activities as chief of state may seem trivial, they showcase national values and lend a warm, human note to the presidency. In fact, Americans objected when President and Mrs. Carter tried to make the office less formal. "We began to receive many complaints that I had gone too far in cutting back the pomp and ceremony," Carter wrote, "so after a few months I authorized the band to play 'Hail to the Chief' on special occasions. I found it to be impressive and enjoyed it."[17]

▶ The President as Political Party Chief

There is no constitutional basis for the President's role as party leader. In 1787, when the Constitution

President Ronald Reagan and First Lady Nancy Reagan greet their dog, Rex, upon their return to the White House in April 1987. White House pets have often helped harried Presidents relax.

was written, the framers could not foresee today's strong political parties. The first to assume this role was President Thomas Jefferson, who was looked to for leadership of his Democratic-Republican party. The President's role as party leader grew in importance as parties gained political power. These are the party activities of modern Presidents:

- helps choose a national party chairperson.
- directs plans for the national nominating convention held every presidential election year.
- helps with the party platform (a document listing the party's policies and positions).
- makes political appointments.
- campaigns for party candidates running for Congress.

- influences same-party members of Congress to vote his way on certain legislation.

Today, the President must play an active leadership role in politics, in order to win the political party's nomination and to get elected to the presidency.

▶ The President as Voice of the People and Protector of the Peace

The presidency has become a "bully pulpit," in Theodore Roosevelt's words, that the President can use to speak to and for Americans. He often promotes principles and programs that he knows are important to the people, such as family values and ethics in government.

As the country's protector of the peace, the President reassures the people in times of economic stress and natural disaster. Rossiter writes:

> The emergencies that can disturb the peace of the United States seem to grow thicker and more vexing every year, and hardly a week now goes by that the President is not called upon to take forceful steps in behalf of a section or city or group or enterprise that has been hit hard and suddenly by disaster. . . . In every instance the President must take the lead to restore the normal pattern of existence.[18]

▶ The President and the Media

Newspapers, magazines, radio, television, and even computer networks let the President reach out to Americans and to the rest of the world. The

President begins getting his message out to the public while he is still a candidate for the office. After he is elected, the President uses the media to inform the public and to help them decide which actions they want the President and Congress to take. According to political consultant Samuel L. Popkin, one presidential speech to the public has as much influence on the national plan of action as twenty-five network news stories.[19]

▶ The President as Chief Economist

The Constitution gives Congress the authority in economic matters, but the President influences the national economy in each of his many roles.

- As chief executive, the President directs the executive department agencies that carry out the spending and taxing decisions made by Congress. He also makes important economic appointments, such as budget director and members of the Federal Reserve Board.

- As chief legislator, the President proposes spending and tax legislation. In addition, he uses the veto to influence which economic bills become law.

- As commander in chief, the President oversees the multibillion-dollar purchases of the Defense Department.

- As chief diplomat, the President negotiates with foreign governments on trade, currency, and other economic matters.

- As chief of state, the President influences the

attitudes of the American people toward government spending and trade.

- As party leader, the President's economic leadership can help or hurt the party's candidates.

Voters most often elect a President they believe can make the country prosper. However, the President's ability to influence the economy is limited by four factors.[20] First, the President shares economic power with others, including Congress, the Federal Reserve Board, the Office of Management and Budget, the Council of Economic Advisors, and the Treasury Department.

Second, economics is a complex subject. Some Presidents understand it better than others, and some have been more interested in it than others.

Third, economic information is not exact, and often reaches the President months after it is collected—too late for him to plan fiscal policies that can make a difference to the nation's economy.

Finally, there are many forces outside the federal government that influence the economy. State and local government policies are not always the same as those of the federal government. Global influences, such as the price of oil or foreign trade policies, are not under the President's control. Large corporations make business decisions that affect the economy, as when IBM, AT&T, and other American businesses laid off thousands of workers in the 1990s. Even the weather may have an affect on the economy, if crops fail in a drought, or if floods and tornadoes destroy property.

The American public tends to blame or praise Presidents for the state of the nation's economy. However, because so many factors are involved, a President who makes all the right decisions will not always cause prosperity. On the other hand, an inexperienced President who sometimes makes poor choices probably will not single-handedly cause a national economic disaster.

Life in the White House

Forty Presidents and their families have lived in the White House, at 1600 Pennsylvania Avenue, Washington, D.C. Some of those Presidents enjoyed the experience more than others. Grover Cleveland complained often of the lack of privacy. President Taft called the White House "the loneliest place in the world."[1] Woodrow Wilson admitted to feeling "a very holy and very terrible isolation" while a resident there.[2] President Harry Truman called the executive mansion "a great white prison."[3]

President Truman also claimed the White House was haunted. After his election he moved alone into the mansion, before his family joined him. In a letter to his wife, Bess, written shortly after he became President, Truman said: "I sit here in this old house and work on foreign affairs, read reports, and work on speeches—all the while listening to the ghosts walk up and down the hallway and even right in here in the study. The floors pop and the drapes move back and forth—I can just imagine old Andy and Teddy having an argument over Franklin. Or James Buchanan and Franklin Pierce deciding which was the more useless to the country. And when Millard Fillmore and Chester Arthur join in for place and show the din is almost unbearable."[4]

The rich history of the White House inspires haunting tales.

▶ Building the President's House

The history of the White House goes back to 1790, when Congress passed the Residence Act, giving President George Washington the authority to set up the federal capital. He chose a hilly tract of farm-land and woods above the Potomac River as the site for government headquarters. The capital was originally called the Federal City, but the name was changed to Washington, District of Columbia (D.C.), in the early 1800s.

Pierre-Charles L'Enfant, a French engineer, was hired to design and build the President's House and the Capitol Building. L'Enfant proved stubborn and disagreeable, and he was fired. He was replaced by James Hoban, an Irish architect, who submitted the winning drawing in a contest sponsored by the Commissioners of Federal City. Construction of the White House had barely begun when Washington left office in 1797.

President John Adams and his wife, Abigail, moved into the unfinished mansion in November 1800. Servants hung laundry from bare brick walls in the East Room. A wooden bridge led to the front door, and the yard was full of workmen's rubble. Water had to be carried from half a mile away, there was an outdoor privy in the backyard, and there was not enough wood for the mansion's many fireplaces.

In letters to her sister, Abigail Adams described the cold, drafty "great castle":

> The house can be lived in, but there is not a single room finished. We have no fence, yard, or other convenience. . . . The main stairs are not up, and will not be this winter. . . . Yet this is a beautiful spot, capable of every improvement, and the more I view it the more I am delighted with it.[5]

Work on the White House progressed through Thomas Jefferson's administration. In 1809, when President James Madison and his wife, Dolley, moved in, living conditions had improved. The Madisons enjoyed entertaining, and they decorated the mansion attractively. Dolley Madison soon became the most popular hostess in Washington.

▶ The House Destroyed

While First Lady Dolley Madison charmed Washington's social circles, President James Madison fought Great Britain over seizure of American ships on the high seas. Congress finally declared war on Great Britain on June 1, 1812. As the war progressed, American soldiers could not prevent the British from marching on Washington.

On August 24, 1814, President Madison rode out to join the troops. Mrs. Madison asked servants to set the table for 3:00 P.M. dinner as usual, in anticipation of her husband's return. Finally, Mrs. Madison was forced to flee as British troops advanced. She escaped, managing to take with her a few White House papers, furnishings, and personal possessions. Reportedly, two passing citizens volunteered to rescue the White House portrait of George Washington painted by artist Gilbert Stuart.

Invading British soldiers found the President's House unlocked and empty. They ate the meal prepared for the Madisons, then set fire to the Executive Mansion and the Capitol Building.

The Madisons were soon reunited, unharmed, but the White House was gutted by fire—only the stone walls were left standing. George Washington's portrait was later returned to the Madisons. Today it hangs in the East Room of the White House.

▶ Reconstruction

James Hoban, the original builder, was hired to reconstruct the President's House. (The name White House became official in 1901.) Though the outer stone walls were still standing after the fire, most of the mansion had to be rebuilt. Construction began in 1815, and in 1817 President James Monroe and his wife, Elizabeth, moved in.

When the Monroes moved in, the house was again unfinished. On the outside, white paint partially covered the smoke-blackened stone. Inside, though thirty fireplaces were kept burning to dry the walls, plaster was still wet. Wallpaper had not yet been hung, and there were no carpets on the unfinished pine floors. Furniture was sparse.

By the time President John Quincy Adams and his wife, Louisa, moved into the White House in 1825, reconstruction was complete.

Remodeling and modernization of the White House continued throughout the 1800s. The south and north porticos were built in 1824 and 1829, respectively. Under President Andrew Jackson, the East Room was furnished and opened for public functions, and running water and the first indoor water closet were installed in 1833. Gas lighting was introduced in 1848, followed by the first central heating system in 1853. The first telephone was brought to the White House in 1879, during Rutherford B. Hayes's administration. Chester A. Arthur installed an elevator. Wiring for electricity was in place by 1891.

▶ Major Makeovers

Since 1825, the White House has had three major makeovers. The first makeover was done in 1902, while Theodore Roosevelt was President. Thousands of people had trooped through the mansion over the years, and the floors were settling dangerously. In fact, every time there was a party, the floors of the State Dining Room and the East Room were propped up with timbers. In addition, a temporary wooden bridge had been constructed as an exit from the East Room windows to the north driveway, to handle large crowds. On the Family Floor, Theodore and Edith Roosevelt and their six children were crowded into eight rooms, to make space for offices.

To solve the problem of cramped quarters, in 1902 Congress appropriated money to construct a new West Wing, with offices for the President and executive staff. The West Wing was doubled in size in 1909 and enlarged again in 1934.

In 1927, when Calvin Coolidge was President, a third floor was added to the White House. This project created eighteen more rooms, including the sunroom over the south portico labeled the "sky parlor" by Grace Coolidge.

The White House was again in poor condition in 1945, when Vice President Harry Truman became President after the death of Franklin D. Roosevelt. Over the years the constant remodeling and daily wear had weakened the building's old wooden beams and walls. When President Truman's bathtub began sinking into the ceiling of the Red Room, and a leg of his daughter Margaret's piano broke through the floor boards, it was clear that the old house needed serious repairs.

During President Truman's first year in office, Congress had grudgingly released funds for a balcony to be built off the second floor behind the columns of the South Portico. Two years later they set aside $5,400,000 to gut the interior of the White House completely, to dig a new basement, and to replace the wooden framework with steel. While work was in progress, the Trumans moved into Blair House, a government guest house across the street. They moved back into the completely rebuilt White House in 1952.[6]

In 1992, the White House received a facelift when twenty-eight layers of white paint were scraped from the outside walls. After the work was finished, the original sandstone carvings and detail work could be seen. When the paint was removed, soot from the fire of 1812 was still visible on some of the stones.

▶ The President's House Today

The modern-day White House now has 132 rooms, as compared to the original 36. There are 412 doors, 32 bathrooms, 45 chandeliers, 66 sculptures, 492 paintings, and 18 acres of lawns and gardens. The White House has a gymnasium, a bowling alley, a library, and a movie theater.

The mansion has four floors: ground, first, second, and third. The first floor, called the state floor, is open for public tours. It includes the East Room, the Green Room, the Blue Room, the Red Room, and the State Dining Room.

There are seven historic rooms on the second floor, including the Queens' Bedroom, the Lincoln Bedroom and Sitting Room, and a private President's Office. (Abraham Lincoln signed the Emancipation Proclamation in his office, which is now the Lincoln Bedroom.) The First Family's living quarters are also on the second floor. The family quarters measure 5,600 square feet, and include 17 bedrooms and 29 fireplaces.

Additional living quarters, guest bedrooms, and storage areas are located on the third floor.

The ground floor contains offices for the President's physician, and a small clinic with a thirteen-member staff. (Additional medical treatment is available at one of Washington's hospitals.) Also on the ground floor are a dental clinic, barbershop, tailor's shop, cafeteria, laundry rooms, carpenter's shop, painter's shop, and a bomb shelter.

A staff of 115 is required to take care of the mansion and the 18 acres surrounding it.[7] The total

The Eisenhower family in the Entrance Hall of the White House, on December 25, 1957. (From left to right: David, Mamie, Barbara, Mary, John (Ike and Mamie's son), Anne, President Dwight, and Susan.) Mamie Eisenhower's Christmas decorations are visible.

dollar amount appropriated for White House operations is difficult to determine from the complicated federal budget, but as of 1993, was estimated at $150 million.[8]

The White House has been furnished with items bought by the many families who lived there, and with gifts from various sources. Money is also raised from donations to pay for White House furnishings and renovations. The Committee for the Preservation of the White House and the White House Historical Association work together, using private donations to purchase furniture, paintings, and other items for the White House.

President Lyndon B. Johnson's Executive Order 11145, issued in 1964, made the White House a museum. This meant that the executive mansion would have an official curator, and Presidents could no longer remove articles, as some had done in the past.

▶ The Oval Office

The President's offices were moved to the new West Wing in 1902. Before that, the chief executive received official visitors and did his daily paperwork in his office on the second floor of the White House.

The first Oval Office was built in 1909 for President William Howard Taft. Franklin D. Roosevelt moved the Oval Office to its present location in the southeast corner of the West Wing in 1934. Also in the West Wing are the Cabinet Room, the Roosevelt Room, staff offices, conference rooms, and press facilities.

President Gerald Ford sits in the Oval Office with his dog, Liberty, on November 7, 1974.

The East Wing, housing three stories of offices and the first presidential bomb shelter, was constructed during World War II.

▶ The President's Workday

Early Presidents were not expected to interfere too much in government business. Except for hosting levees (formal receptions) for visitors to the White House, Presidents before 1930 had little to do.

Benjamin Harrison's 1890 schedule was typical. His work day began at 9:00 A.M. Official business was read and letters were answered until noon. After lunch, visitors were received for an hour or two, then the President was free for the rest of the day.

Some Presidents took afternoon naps, while others used their free time for exercise and other activities. John Quincy Adams walked early in the morning, and he took an afternoon dip in the Potomac River when weather permitted. Theodore Roosevelt exercised in the afternoon and read in the evenings. Calvin Coolidge was called the "do-nothing" President, because he was seldom in his office.

There were exceptions to the light workload. James K. Polk left office in 1849 with his health undermined from hard work. He died shortly after leaving office, at the age of fifty-three. Abraham Lincoln was overwhelmed with work after the Civil War began, and often received callers until midnight.

The President's workload increased around 1930, when the federal government began to handle more of the nation's problems. Herbert Hoover spent long days in his office during the Great Depression. And worries over the country's economic problems and World War II probably contributed to undermining the health of Franklin D. Roosevelt.

By 1952 the presidency was considered a full-time job. Dwight D. Eisenhower was often criticized for taking occasional afternoons and most weekends off. In defense of his schedule he said, "I believe there is a point at which efficiency is best served. After you spend a certain number of hours at work, you pass your peak of efficiency."[9]

By his own admission, George Bush was "hyper." In just one day of his presidency (April 25, 1989) he signed disaster relief papers for Texas, attended a fund-raising breakfast in San Jose, California, and then gave a speech at a fund-raising luncheon in

Silicon Valley. That afternoon he flew to Orange County to visit the confiscated ranch of an arrested drug dealer. Then he attended a meeting with Hispanic Republicans at UCLA. By this time reporters and aides were drooping. Bush, as fresh as when the day began, ordered the helicopter to take his party to the Angels baseball game. During the game he snacked on boiled shrimp, nachos, hot dogs, and popcorn.[10]

In one typical day in February 1994, President Bill Clinton jogged with Olympic Torchbearers at 7:30 A.M., was briefed in the Oval Office by his staff, attended a bipartisan leadership meeting in the Cabinet Room, met with his Secretary of Labor, presided over a Department of Labor Conference on Reemployment, attended a congressional crime meeting in the Cabinet Room, received guests at a reception in the White House Blue Room, and—finally—spoke in the Grand Foyer that evening.[11]

▶ The First Lady's Workday

Duties of the First Ladies have also increased over the years. Before Mrs. Franklin D. Roosevelt, the official duty of Presidents' wives was to host White House social functions. Eleanor Roosevelt changed the role of First Lady. She entertained, but she also held press conferences, traveled around the country making speeches and radio broadcasts, and wrote a daily newspaper column titled "My Day." President Roosevelt's political enemies criticized the First Lady's activities, but Eleanor Roosevelt was a favorite of the American people.[12]

First Lady Jacqueline Kennedy was also an energetic figure. She won the sympathy and admiration of the world after her husband's assassination. In 1968, she married Greek businessman Aristotle Onassis. From 1978 until her death in 1994, Mrs. Kennedy Onassis lived in New York City and worked as a book editor.[13]

Rosalynn Carter, wife of President Jimmy Carter, also worked hard as First Lady. In her autobiography, *First Lady From Plains*, she reported that during her first fourteen months in the White House she visited 18 nations and 27 U.S. cities, held 259 private meetings and 50 public meetings, made 15 major speeches, held 22 press conferences, gave 32 interviews, had 77 hours of briefings, attended 83 official receptions, held 26 special-interest and group meetings at the White House, spent more than 300 hours working in mental health, received 152,000 letters and 7,939 invitations, signed 150 photographs a week, and made 16 public appearances around Washington, D.C.[14]

Biographers have said that Nancy Reagan wielded more power than any other First Lady in history, but Hillary Rodham Clinton, wife of President Bill Clinton, has perhaps attracted the most attention for her role in government. An accomplished attorney, Mrs. Clinton headed a presidential task force that wrote a complex plan for changing the nation's health care programs. Critics disliked Mrs. Clinton's assertive style and her involvement in official decisions.[15]

▶ Presidential Salaries and Expenses

Through the 1800s the President's salary was $25,000 a year. Out of this amount he paid salaries to his personal secretary and household servants, and he paid for food and drink for his family and guests. Many of the nation's less wealthy Presidents left office in debt.

Since 1969, the President of the United States has received an annual salary of $200,000. He also has a taxable expense account of $50,000 and a nontaxable travel expense account, not to exceed $100,000 annually. The President's pay seems modest when compared to corporate executives in the private sector, but the many fringe benefits that have been added over the years now total millions of dollars.

The government pays White House utility bills, and pays for official entertaining, such as state dinners honoring foreign rulers. The President pays for daily meals for his family and their personal guests, and for private receptions and parties.

Although the President receives a travel allowance, for security reasons he seldom uses public transportation. A fleet of limousines is at his disposal, including an armor-plated model with a detachable roof. A Marine Corps helicopter, Marine One, is set aside for the President's use. The President, his family, and staff also have exclusive use of a modified Boeing 747 called Air Force One, which can carry 80 passengers and a crew of 23. It reportedly costs $41,875 an hour to fly, not counting maintenance and support personnel.[16] Inside Air Force One are desks, couches, beds, medical and food service facilities, and communications equipment. Traditionally, the President's family members and invited guests have been asked to pay their own way to travel on Air Force One.

The Former Presidents Act of 1958 gave the outgoing President a pension of $50,000 a year. By the time President George Bush left office in 1993, former Presidents received government pensions of $148,000 a year.[17] In addition, Bush received $1.5 million to use in his transition to the life of a private citizen.[18] Each also receives $150,000 a year for the first thirty months after leaving office and $96,000 annually thereafter, to pay for personal staff. The government pays to maintain presidential libraries for ex-Presidents, and also pays for postage for nonpolitical correspondence, a furnished office, and Secret Service protection.[19]

▶ Protecting the President

In the early days of the presidency, huge crowds of visitors trooped through the White House. Joanna Rucker, James K. Polk's niece, complained that even the first family's living quarters were not private: "The house belongs to the Government and everyone feels at home and they sometimes stalk into our bedroom and say they are looking at the house."[20]

As more citizens flocked to see the President, the danger to his personal safety increased. In 1835, President Andrew Jackson was confronted by a deranged man with two pistols. After both guns misfired, Jackson hit the attacker with his cane and drove him off. Franklin Pierce witnessed this assassination attempt at the Capitol. Later, after he became President, Pierce hired the first presidential bodyguard.

In 1865, Lincoln signed into law a bill creating the Secret Service within the Treasury Department. The Secret Service was formed to reduce the counterfeiting of U.S. currency. The protection of the President and Vice President and their families became the service's permanent function in 1951. Since that time, the protection of the Secret Service has been extended to include candidates for the presidency and foreign dignitaries visiting the United States.

Today specially trained agents of the Secret Service guard the President and Vice President and their families around the clock.

Sometimes Presidents and their families find it difficult to live a normal life, always under guard. President Carter told of his concern for his then nine-year-old daughter, Amy, as she attended her first day of public school in Washington, D.C.:

> It was wrenching to see her on the evening news, a tiny figure with a heavy bag, struggling toward the school door through a mass of television cameras and news reporters and surrounded by a crowd of security agents and onlookers.[21]

▶ Assassinations and Threats

Threats against the President were not as common in the 1800s as they are today. However, Presidents

Lincoln, Garfield, and McKinley all were killed while in office. Lincoln was shot on April 14, 1865, by John Wilkes Booth, an actor who thought he was saving the South. Garfield was shot on July 2, 1881, by a disgruntled attorney seeking a government job. Mortally wounded, the President died on September 19. McKinley was standing in a reception line at the 1901 Buffalo Pan-American Exposition when extremist Leon F. Czolgosz shot him twice. He died eight days later.

Abraham Lincoln and his family were usually guarded by a District of Columbia police officer. On the night President Lincoln was shot, the guard had wandered off. Neither Presidents Garfield nor McKinley had bodyguards nearby when they were killed.

John F. Kennedy is the only President to have been assassinated since the Secret Service began protecting the President. He was shot by Lee Harvey Oswald on November 22, 1963, while riding through Dallas, Texas, in a motorcade. He was the youngest U.S. President ever elected and, at forty-six, the youngest to die in office.

In spite of the tight security around Presidents, assassination attempts continue to occur. On the afternoon of November 1, 1950, two Puerto Rican nationalists, Griselio Torresola and Oscar Collazo, shot two guards in an attempt to enter Blair House, where Harry Truman was napping in an upstairs bedroom. One of the guards, though dying, shot and killed Torresola. Secret Service agents wounded

Collazo. The President was unharmed. Truman later commuted Collazo's death sentence. President Carter gave him clemency.[22]

In September of 1975, two separate attempts were made on Gerald Ford's life. In Sacramento, California, Lynette "Squeaky" Fromme, a follower of cult leader Charles Manson, was captured by Secret Service agents after pointing a gun at the President. No one was injured. Seventeen days later, in San Francisco, Sara Jane Moore fired a gun at President Ford as he waved to the crowd outside a hotel. Moore's aim was deflected by an alert bystander, and the shot missed President Ford and ricocheted off the front of the hotel.[23] Both Fromme and Moore are still in prison.

On March 30, 1981, John Hinckley, Jr., fired a gun at Ronald Reagan as the President left the Hilton Hotel in Washington, D.C. A bullet entered Reagan's body under his left arm, hit a rib, traveled through his lung, and came to rest inches from his heart. The President was quickly taken to George Washington University Hospital.

No one died that day, but James Brady, the President's press secretary, was seriously wounded and permanently disabled when a bullet entered his skull. Secret Service agent Tim McCarthy was shot in the chest, and police officer Tom Delehanty was shot in the neck. Hinckley was captured at the scene by Secret Service agents. He was tried, found not guilty by reason of insanity, and confined to a psychiatric hospital, where he remains today.[24]

Two disturbing events occurred during President Bill Clinton's time in office. In September 1994, Frank Eugene Corder killed himself when he crashed a stolen Cessna airplane into the south side of the White House. Though the Clintons were home when the plane crashed, no one else was injured.[25] In November 1994, Francisco Martin Duran was charged with attempting to assassinate President Clinton after he fired an assault rifle at the White House. The Clintons were away at the time, and no one was injured in the attempt.[26]

▶ Presidential Privileges

Tight security and constant media attention are bothersome aspects of the job. But Presidents have perquisites that ordinary citizens do not. Everyone addresses the President as "Mr. President." Members of the military must salute their commander in chief. "Hail to the Chief," a special march, is played whenever the President appears in public. (This custom was introduced by Sara Polk when her husband was President.) New books and movies are sent to the White House for the enjoyment of the first family. Many entertainers waive their fees for the honor of performing for the President. Tennis courts, a swimming pool, and a bowling alley are provided for the First Family's recreational use.

A vacation home in Maryland's Catoctin Mountains, named Camp David after President Dwight D. Eisenhower's grandson, is available for the First Family when they want to get away from Washington. The retreat includes ten cabins, a lodge, a conference

President Jimmy Carter rides a bicycle with his family at Camp David, September 6, 1980. (First Lady Rosalynn Carter is in the background.)

room that holds fifty people, a presidential office, a projection theater, a skeet range, basketball courts, and a trampoline.

Some observers fear that Presidents are treated too much like royalty. In *The Twilight of the Presidency*, George E. Reedy, former press secretary and special assistant to President Lyndon Johnson, warns that when Presidents are treated as kings, they can become too isolated; and when Presidents become isolated, their decisions suffer:

> In retrospect, it seems little short of amazing that President Kennedy would ever have embarked upon the ill-fated Bay of Pigs venture . . . It was poorly conceived, poorly planned, poorly executed,

and undertaken with grossly inadequate knowledge. . . . White House councils are not debating
matches in which ideas emerge from the heated ex-
changes of participants. The council centers
around the President himself, to whom everyone
addresses his observations.[27]

Somehow the office must be made "human"
again, Reedy concludes. The President must:

plunge into the world of reality. . . walk the streets
that real men and women walk . . . breathe the air
that real men and women breathe.[28]

In modern society, Reedy admits, this may be
impossible.

Supporting the President

When John Adams was Vice President, he complained to his wife, Abigail, "My country has in its wisdom contrived for me the most insignificant office that ever the invention of man contrived or his imagination conceived."[1]

A century and a half later, Franklin D. Roosevelt's first Vice President, John N. ("Cactus Jack") Garner, told Lyndon Johnson that the job "ain't worth a cup of warm spit."[2]

▶ The Vice President

The Vice President's job has become more meaningful over the years. However, according to President George Bush, who served as Vice President under Ronald Reagan, "The job doesn't lend itself to high profile and decision making. It lends itself to loyally supporting the president of the United States, giving him your best judgment, and then when the president makes a decision, supporting it."[3]

The Constitution lists just two functions for the Vice President of the United States: to serve as President of the Senate, voting only in case of a tie, and to take over as President if for any reason the elected chief executive cannot serve.

Vice Presidents in the 1800s and early 1900s were seldom included in policy-making decisions. Except for attending various state ceremonies, they had little to do.

Vice Presidents since World War II have had more responsibility. Vice President Walter Mondale toured Europe and Japan to show that the Carter administration considered the continued cooperation of these nations important. Vice President George Bush traveled more than a million miles and visited seventy countries, representing the United States and President Reagan. As part of his "reinventing government" initiative, Vice President Al Gore called for deep cuts in the cost of running the government, including the elimination of 252,000 federal jobs.

The size of the Vice President's staff has increased with the importance of the office. In 1959, Vice President Richard Nixon's staff totaled fewer than twenty. Vice President George Bush had a staff of some seventy members. Today the Vice President's inner staff almost duplicates that of the President.

The formal office of the Vice President is located in the old Executive Office Building, across the street from the White House. This office is used mainly for ceremonial occasions. The Vice President's second, working office is located in the West Wing of the White House. He has a third office on Capitol Hill, for his use as presiding officer of the Senate.

Congress did not appropriate funds to maintain an official residence for the Vice President until 1974. At that time they designated the Admiral's House, on the grounds of the Naval Observatory in Washington, D.C., as the Vice President's residence. The house has twelve rooms, plus several service areas and six bathrooms. Walter Mondale was the first Vice President to live in the house.

John Adams, the first Vice President, earned $5,000 a year. By 1993, the Vice President's pay had risen to $171,500 annually, with an additional taxable expense account of $10,000.

Albert Gore, Jr., shown here in 1993, served as Vice President under Bill Clinton.

President Lyndon Johnson at a luncheon meeting of the AFL-CIO Committee on Political Education in 1968. Vice President Hubert Humphrey is seated in the background.

Before ratification of the Twenty-fifth Amendment in 1967, there was no provision in the Constitution for filling the job of Vice President if it became vacant between elections. Under the Twenty-fifth Amendment, whenever a vacancy occurs in the vice presidency, the President appoints a Vice President. The appointed Vice President takes office after confirmation by a majority vote of both houses of Congress.

▶ Executive Office of the President

Executive Order 8248, issued by President Franklin D. Roosevelt in 1939, created the Executive Office of the President (EOP). The EOP was created to help the President with budgeting, personnel management, planning, and decision-making.

The composition of the EOP varies with each presidential administration. In 1994, the EOP included the following agencies: White House Office, Council of Economic Advisors, National Security Council, Office of Management and Budget, Council of Environmental Quality, Office of Policy Development, Office of the U.S. Trade Representative, Office of Science and Technology Policy, National Critical Materials Council, Office of National Drug Control Policy, and Office of Administration.

▶ White House Office

White House Office staff members are the President's closest assistants. The staff may be organized in any way the President wants it to be. Staff members have no government employment status or tenure, and they can be reassigned or dismissed for any reason at any time. They handle the documents, correspondence, and appeals for help that flood the White House. They also convey the President's policies to other executive agencies, the media, and the general public. The President appoints all White House Office staff members. These appointments do not require congressional approval.

Early Presidents hired personal secretaries and paid them from their own pockets. Throughout the 1800s secretaries and aides fulfilled the President's needs for scheduling, political advice, office management, and public relations. Presidents borrowed employees from other government agencies whenever they needed more help.

Franklin D. Roosevelt's administration marked the beginning of today's staff system. Roosevelt won authorization from Congress to hire a larger, permanent staff that worked only for him. President Roosevelt had twelve personal aides. During his administration, there were fewer than sixty-five full-time White House employees.[4]

By the time Franklin D. Roosevelt's term in office ended, the President needed a larger, more specialized staff. In 1947, President Truman's staff numbered about two hundred. The White House Office staff also became more structured during Truman's presidency, including, among others, a press secretary, appointments secretary, personnel director, special counsel, legislative drafter, military aides, and speechwriters.

Over the years, the White House Office staff increased as Presidents concentrated resources and power within the White House. Though some Presidents have tried to reduce the size of the White House Office staff, few have succeeded. Presidents from Richard Nixon through Bill Clinton had large, specialized staffs. As of July 1994, President Bill Clinton's White House Office staff numbered 391, and the total number of EOP employees was 1,615.[5]

The White House Office staff can add to the President's success in office, or it can cause problems for the President. For example, both John F. Kennedy and Lyndon Johnson benefited from an efficient staff. However, less capable staff members probably contributed to the Watergate and Iran-Contra scandals that troubled the Nixon and Reagan administrations.

The most important positions within the White House Office are chief of staff, special counsel, national security advisor, press secretary, domestic policy advisor, and personnel office director.

Chief of Staff. The chief of staff is the gate-keeper and hatchet-wielder for the President, screening visitors and deciding which matters can be handled by an assistant. The chief of staff also does the dirty work for the President, such as firing or reprimanding other employees.

Because the chief of staff can deny access to the President, he is not always well liked. President Jimmy Carter wrote that Hamilton Jordan, his chief of staff, "was more seriously misunderstood and underestimated by the press and public than anyone else who worked in my administration."[6] John Sununu, chief of staff for President George Bush, earned a reputation for being "hostile, brash, and rude."[7]

Special Counsel. The special counsel is the attorney to the President and the White House. He or she is consulted when the President wants to know if certain actions, proposed legislation, and treaties are legal. The special counsel's office also oversees security clearances for presidential appointees.

Domestic Policy Advisor. The domestic policy advisor settles disputes between agencies within the

United States government. This person also advises the President on domestic matters, and helps draft domestic legislation. Some functions overlap with those of the national security advisor.

Press Secretary. The press secretary is in close daily contact with the chief executive, informing the media and the public about the President's position on domestic and foreign issues. This person becomes familiar to the public as the President's spokesperson on television.

The White House communications office functions separately from that of the press secretary, but also handles requests for information from journalists. This office sends out press releases promoting the President's views on issues, and otherwise pushes the President's agenda.

National Security Advisor. The national security advisor is the President's chief counsel on foreign policy. This person also guides operations of the National Security Council.

The Personnel Office. Most members of the President's inner staff are selected from among friends and former aides. However, qualified candidates are needed for the many other appointments the President must make. The White House personnel office conducts searches for potential office-holders. Once they are located, this office checks on qualifications, conducts interviews, and works with the White House special counsel on background checks. When a suitable candidate for appointment is found, the personnel office presents the nominee to the President. If necessary, the candidate's name is sent to the Senate for approval. Personnel office staff might also brief the appointee on questions to expect from the Senate.

▶ The Outer Circle

White House Office staff members make up the President's inner circle. Other agencies within the Executive Office of the President form the outer circle—they are further removed from the President. The directors of these agencies are also appointed by the President. Unlike appointees within the White House Office, they are subject to Senate approval. These are five of the ten agencies within the President's outer circle:

Office of Management and Budget (OMB). All departments and agencies of the executive branch must submit annual budget requests to the OMB. The OMB prepares an annual budget for submission to Congress, which makes this agency an important managerial and agenda-setting tool of the President.

National Security Council (NSC). The National Security Council was created by the National Security Act of 1947. The NSC advises the President about U.S., military, and foreign security. This agency also directs operations of the Central Intelligence Agency.

The NSC is made up of the President, the Vice President, the Secretary of State, and the Secretary of Defense. The chairman of the Joint Chiefs of Staff and the director of the Central Intelligence Agency also act as advisors to the NSC.

Office of Policy Development (OPD). Unlike other agencies within the EOP, the Office of Policy Development is staffed entirely by presidential appointees. The office is headed by the domestic policy advisor. The OPD's job is to alert the President to important domestic issues. The agency also evaluates policies in operation, and helps write domestic legislation for submission to Congress.

Council of Economic Advisors (CEA). The Council of Economic Advisors was created by the 1946 Employment Act. The three-member appointed council helps the President determine where the nation's economy is heading, and helps him prepare his annual economic report to Congress.

Office of the U.S. Trade Representative. The trade office is directed by the U.S. trade representative (USTR), a cabinet-level appointee with ambassador status. The USTR meets with the heads of foreign nations to discuss trade, and advises the President on all aspects of international commerce. Issues handled by the USTR include expansion of U.S. exports, unfair trade practices, and U.S. policy on any issue involving international trade.

▶ The Cabinet

Not only is the Cabinet not mentioned in the Constitution, it was never provided for in any law passed by Congress. George Washington started the practice of meeting with his cabinet, which consisted of his attorney general and the secretaries of the departments of State, Treasury, and War. Today's cabinet includes the President, the Vice President, the secretaries of each of the fourteen executive or cabinet departments, and any other official the President wants to invite. The President appoints each cabinet secretary, subject to Senate confirmation.

Some Presidents met often with their cabinets. In the beginning of his term, Harry Truman often asked his cabinet to vote on important issues. Later, however, he relied on a smaller, more informal group of advisors. Dwight D. Eisenhower often discussed issues with his cabinet before taking action. According to Stephen E. Ambrose, in *Eisenhower—The President*, "Eisenhower felt that this trait was a source of strength. He wanted to hear every legitimate point of view, to take all possible repercussions into account, before acting."[8]

Other Presidents did not work closely with their cabinets. John F. Kennedy found he could work more efficiently with members of his White House Office staff. President Jimmy Carter accepted the resignations of many members of his cabinet in 1979, when his administration appeared to lack focus, and he had lost control over his cabinet.

▶ Executive Departments

The fourteen executive or cabinet departments are the largest agencies within the executive branch of the government. They include:

- Department of Agriculture
- Department of Commerce
- Department of Defense

- Department of Education
- Department of Energy
- Department of Heath and Human Services
- Department of Housing and Urban Development
- Department of Interior
- Department of Justice
- Department of Labor
- Department of State
- Department of Transportation
- Department of the Treasury
- Department of Veterans' Affairs

These are seven of the largest and most prominent executive departments:

Department of Defense. The Department of Defense is the largest executive department. It was established by the National Security Act of 1947, and was given cabinet status in 1949. This department maintains and directs the nation's military and defense forces.

A civilian (nonmilitary) secretary heads the Department of Defense. Each branch of the military is organized separately under its own secretary. The civilian secretaries of the Army, Navy, Marine Corps, and Air Force are responsible to the secretary of defense. (The Coast Guard is under the authority of the Department of Transportation.)

The military departments are coordinated by the Joint Chiefs of Staff. The top military members of the Joint Chiefs of Staff include the chairman, chiefs of staff of the Army, Navy, and Air Force, and commandant of the Marine Corps.

After the President, the Secretary of Defense has the final say in military decisions. The secretary makes recommendations to the President about personnel and weapons needs, and about the military capacity of foreign foes.

Department of Health and Human Services. HHS was established in 1979, to replace the Department of Health, Education and Welfare. It is the second largest cabinet department, next to Defense. This department is more closely involved in the daily lives of American citizens than is any other cabinet department. Its employees mail out Social Security checks, make payments for health care under the

A Park Service Ranger, of the Department of the Interior, leads a tour of Alcatraz Prison.

Medicare and Medicaid programs, and distribute food stamps to Americans with low incomes.

HHS includes the Public Health Service, headed by the Surgeon General. The Public Health Service funds health research, collects health statistics, and protects consumers from unsafe foods and drugs. Agencies within the Public Health Service that carry out these duties include the Centers for Disease Control (CDC), the National Center for Health Statistics, and the Food and Drug Administration (FDA).

Department of Justice. The Department of Justice, established in 1870, is headed by the attorney general, who was given cabinet rank in 1789. Seven assistant attorneys general head the following divisions within the department: offices and services, antitrust, civil, civil rights, criminal, land and natural resources, and tax.

The Department of Justice represents the United States government in legal matters. It enforces civil rights laws and all federal criminal laws, except those specifically assigned to other agencies. The Federal Bureau of Investigation (FBI), the International Criminal Police Organization called INTERPOL, Immigration and Naturalization Service (INS), and the Drug Enforcement Administration (DEA) are major investigative agencies within the Department of Justice.

Department of Labor. In 1913, President William H. Taft signed a bill to establish a cabinet-level department to help American wage earners. Today the department enforces hundreds of laws dealing with workers' unemployment insurance, minimum wages and overtime pay, occupational health and safety, antidiscrimination in employment, pension rights, job training, and collective bargaining.

The department's Employment and Training Office operates the Job Corps. The office also administers programs responsible for work training and employment and unemployment services.

Department of State. One of the oldest executive departments, the Department of State was formed in 1781 as the Department of Foreign Affairs. It was named the Department of State in 1789, and it directs and coordinates U.S. foreign relations. Ambassadors within the State Department represent the United States in 155 countries around the world.

The secretary of state is the highest-ranking department secretary in the President's cabinet, and is a member of the National Security Council.

Department of the Treasury. The Treasury Department was established by the first session of Congress in 1789. Its first secretary was Alexander Hamilton. The Treasury Department supervises the financial resources of the United States. Agencies within the department collect income taxes, manufacture paper currency and coins, enforce tax and tariff laws, direct anticounterfeiting operations, and provide protection for certain government executives. Included within the Treasury Department are the Bureau of Alcohol, Tobacco and Firearms (ATF), Bureau of Customs, Bureau of Engraving and Printing, Financial Management

Service, Bureau of Internal Revenue, and the Secret Service.

Department of Veterans' Affairs. The Veterans' Administration, created in 1930, became the Department of Veterans' Affairs in 1989, under President Ronald Reagan. The Department of Veterans' Affairs was the last of the fourteen executive departments created. The DVA provides disability payments, education and training, home loan assistance, insurance, and health care for military veterans. It also operates 111 national veterans' cemeteries.

Other Cabinet Members. In addition to the fourteen executive department secretaries, the President often names other government officials to the cabinet. For example, President Bill Clinton gave cabinet-level status to his Office of Management and Budget director, U.S. Trade representative, United Nations representative, Environmental Protection Agency director, director of Council of Economic Advisers, chief White House science advisor, and director of the National Security Council.[9]

Independent Agencies and Commissions

In 1816, the top civilian members of the executive branch included President James Madison, Vice President George Clinton, and five cabinet secretaries. Nevertheless, that year Thomas Jefferson wrote in a letter to a friend, "I think we have more machinery of government than is necessary."[1]

Today, Jefferson would be amazed. The President is now responsible for the Executive Office of the President. He is also responsible for more than sixty major independent executive agencies, and more than two hundred and fifty commissions.

▶ Independent Agencies

Independent agencies within the executive branch are formed when Congress or the President wants to focus special attention on an issue or problem, outside of the usual presidential organization. Independent executive branch agencies may be set up inside or outside of the cabinet departments, but they have the authority to act on their own. For example, the National Aeronautics and Space Administration (NASA) was set up outside a specific department, and it operates independently.

Two other agencies that are part of cabinet departments but act independently are the Federal Bureau of Investigation in the Department of Justice, and the Internal Revenue Service in the Department of the Treasury.

As an independent agency, the National Aeronautics and Space Administration (NASA) promotes space exploration.

Independent agencies are created in one of three ways: by an act of Congress, by an Executive Order issued by the President, or by joint action of Congress and the President.

The President appoints directors or commissioners to head independent agencies. Some appointees serve at the discretion of the President. Others, even though appointed by the President, cannot by dismissed by him.

There are three types of independent agencies: regulatory agencies, executive agencies, and government corporations.

▶ Regulatory Agencies

Regulatory agencies within the executive branch check on the health and safety of workers in certain occupations and industries. They also protect American consumers. Because Congress did not want the chief executive to have too much influence on regulatory agencies, they are not directly responsible to the President.

Regulatory agencies may require businesses to inform the public about their products, such as ingredient lists on foods, and health warnings on tobacco and alcohol products. Some agencies have the power to recall consumer products that are considered dangerous to users. Some, like the Federal Communications Commission, may require special licenses or registration. For instance, physicians must obtain a registration number from the Drug Enforcement Administration to dispense or prescribe certain restricted drugs.

Regulatory agencies may also make inspections, and they may levy fines or start court proceedings for violations of the law. For example, inspectors with the Department of Labor's Mine Safety and Health Administration check metal, nonmetal, and coal mines for worker safety. MSHA inspectors write citations that can lead to fines for violators.

Other major independent regulatory agencies include the Consumer Product Safety Commission (CPSC), Interstate Commerce Commission (ICC), Federal Reserve Board (FRB), National Labor Relations Board (NLRB), Federal Communications Commission (FCC), Federal Trade Commission (FTC), Civil Aeronautics Board (CAB), and Securities and Exchange Commission (SEC).

Examples of regulatory agencies functioning within existing cabinet departments are the Food and Drug Administration (FDA) in the Department of Health and Human Services, and the Occupational Safety and Health Administration (OSHA) in the Department of Labor.

▶ Independent Executive Agencies

Independent executive agencies are not part of a cabinet department. Unlike independent regulatory agencies, executive agencies report directly to the President. Examples of the most influential executive agencies include the National Aeronautics and Space Administration (NASA) and the Environmental Protection Agency (EPA).

Sometimes independent executive agencies are created to get things done more quickly and more efficiently than existing agencies, while remaining free from the usual government controls and pressures. The Environmental Protection Agency (EPA), for example, was made independent of any other agency or department that might have environmental interests.

▶ Government Corporations

A third type of independent agency within the executive branch is the government corporation. Government corporations operate outside the cabinet departments. They function much like private companies selling services. The U.S. Postal Service became a government corporation in 1970. (Before that it had cabinet status.) Other government corporations include the Tennessee Valley Authority (TVA), set up to sell electric power, and the Amtrak passenger train service.

Investors in government corporations do not own stock or receive dividends, but government corporations can use the profits made in doing business. They must submit regular reports to Congress and the President.

▶ Presidential Commissions

The President may establish a commission to gather information or to focus attention on an issue that is outside the scope of other agencies.

George Washington appointed the first presidential commission, to investigate the Whiskey Rebellion. In the summer of 1794, farmers in western Pennsylvania refused to pay federal excise taxes

The United States Postal Service, a government corporation, sells its services. Clerks read and key in ZIP Codes to sort large flat envelopes and magazines on a flat sorting machine.

on whiskey they made from their own grain. The farmers earned most of their income from their whiskey, and they believed that the federal government had no right to tax it. George Washington ordered 15,000 troops to Pennsylvania to enforce the tax law. The riots ended when the leaders were arrested.

Every President since Washington has appointed special commissions. President Lyndon Johnson's 1968 Commission on Income Maintenance considered a guaranteed annual income for low-income Americans.[2] The Presidential Commission on the

Human Immunodeficiency Virus Epidemic (AIDS Commission) was formed in the late 1980s.[3]

Commissions can be created by Congress or the President. They are usually placed within the executive office. The three types of presidential commissions are permanent advisory groups, ad hoc commissions, and White House conferences.

▶ Permanent Advisory Organizations

When Presidents want advice from experts outside the White House or the Cabinet, they can appoint a permanent advisory organization (committee, commission, council, board, or task force). Permanent advisory organizations study an issue for an indefinite period of time. They report regularly to the President.

Permanent advisory organizations are assigned in one of three ways. They can be made independent, can be placed within the Executive Office of the President, or they can be located in one of the cabinet departments. For example, the Advisory Committee on Federal Pay is independent. The President's Task Force on Legal Equity for Women is located in the Executive Office of the President. The President's Council on Physical Fitness and Sports is part of the Department of Health and Human Services.

▶ Ad Hoc Commissions

Ad hoc means "formed for a specific purpose." Ad hoc commissions are appointed to investigate one certain issue. They may meet for up to a three-year period, but no longer. Ad hoc commissions are made up of government employees, private citizens, or experts in a certain field, such as business or medicine. They are strictly advisory, and they have no authority to act on their findings.

Examples of ad hoc commissions include the following:

- The Warren Commission, also called the President's Commission on the Assassination of President Kennedy.

- The National Commission on the Causes and Prevention of Violence (also known as the Eisenhower Commission).

- The Tower Commission, formed to investigate the involvement of the White House in the Iran-Contra affair during President Ronald Reagan's administration.[4]

White House Conferences. White House conferences are temporary, lasting from one day to several days. Conferences may be huge events, or they may be attended by just a few persons. They address one issue or concern. Participants are invited to attend. They either meet directly with the President, or they report to him at the end of the conference.

In 1966 President Lyndon Johnson asked five Mexican-American leaders to join him for a conference, after learning that Mexican Americans felt ignored by his administration. The group met with the President's aides in the White House cafeteria. After the meeting, President Johnson conducted a tour of the White House. As a result of the conference, Mexican-American leader Vincente Ximenes was appointed to the Equal Opportunity Commission.[5]

Independent executive branch agencies and commissions sometimes get faster results than do larger government agencies. For example, it can take years for Congress to study how to cut the cost of running the government, and then to pass laws for that purpose. During President Ronald Reagan's administration, the 170-member Grace Commission met for one year (a relatively short period of time in government terms), then turned in a list of 2,478 ways to cut the cost of government. Thirteen hundred of the commission's suggestions were soon put to use, saving the government (and taxpayers) $39 million.[6]

The Changing Presidency

Article II of the Constitution provided for a President of the United States who would not always be dominated by Congress, but would have power of his own. In wording Article II as they did, the framers of the Constitution also provided for growth and change of the presidency over time.

▶ Growth in the President's Power

In *The American Presidency*, Clinton Rossiter explains that the growth in the power of the presidency over the years has not been steady, but has varied with the person in office. The modern presidency, however, is much more powerful than it was in George Washington's time. Today, in Rossiter's words, the presidency "cuts deeply into the powers of Congress . . . It cuts deeply into the lives of the people."[1] (See chapter 2 for an explanation of the President's powers.)

The presidency becomes more powerful each time Congress gives more authority to the executive branch. According to Constitution expert Donald L. Robinson, in *"To the Best of My Ability"—The Presidency and the Constitution*, Congress has yielded power to the President for two reasons:[2]

First, Congress was not set up to act quickly or secretly, but to debate issues openly and carefully before making decisions. Because national economic and security problems often demand fast or secret action, Congress gave the President the power to act more quickly. Thomas Jefferson could send the Navy to roust Barbary pirates harassing American ships. Richard Nixon was given the authority to impose wage and price controls whenever he considered them necessary to control inflation. George Bush was able to order U.S. Marines to Somalia, to help protect food shipments delivered to the starving population.

A second reason that Congress has gradually given more authority to the President is that Senators and Representatives often become experts in certain areas, such as banking, agriculture, or energy, but they seldom have the time to develop a general viewpoint. The President, on the other hand, generally has a broad national plan of action. Therefore, Congress has created or approved departments and agencies within the executive branch to help the President accomplish broad goals.

▶ Accomplishments of the Presidents

Each of the forty-two men who have held the office of President has used his authority in different ways, and each has contributed toward making the office what it is today.

Lists of "great" Presidents differ, because presidential scholars do not always agree. However, the eight Presidents listed below are often credited as strong Presidents who in some way changed the presidency for those who came after them. Rossiter lists these eight, plus six more, who, he claims, "strengthened" the presidency:[3]

George Washington is listed among the notable Presidents because he was the first man to fill the office, and because he was widely admired for his dignity and integrity. As George Bush once wrote,"In

President Bill Clinton was inaugurated in January 1993. Each President has contributed toward making the office what it is today.

matters of substance as well as of protocol—George Washington helped define the office of President of the United States. It was a task that has been taken on by each of his successors, in turn."⁴

As the first President, Washington set important precedents for later Presidents. For example, he used the presidential veto—a major tool of the presidency—for the first time in 1792, when he turned down legislation passed by Congress. He also set a precedent for the use of martial law.

Washington was also a leader in setting foreign policy. For instance, when the French Revolution led to war between France and England, he insisted that the United States remain neutral, until the country could grow stronger.

When he left office after his second term, Washington warned against too much political party involvement, and against long-term unions with foreign nations.

Thomas Jefferson was a strong political and legislative leader. His purchase of the Louisiana Territory set a precedent for adding new land, even though the Constitution made no such provision. His presidency also marked the beginning of the President as political party leader. Jefferson's presidency was followed by twenty years of dominance by Congress.

Andrew Jackson took office in 1829, and he reasserted presidential authority. He ordered troops to Charleston, South Carolina, when that state voted to nullify (cancel) federal tariff laws. South Carolina also threatened to secede, to withdraw from the Union, if the government tried to collect the taxes. Congress supported Jackson by passing the Force Bill, authorizing the President to use troops to collect federal taxes. Before any fighting began, Jackson agreed to a compromise. The tariff was lowered, and South Carolina dropped nullification legislation.[5]

Abraham Lincoln entered the White House in 1861, and he benefited from Jackson's strong presidency. Faced with the nation's first and only Civil War, Lincoln took control. He set the pattern for Presidents who came after him to use their emergency powers in times of crisis.

Theodore Roosevelt is hailed as a strong President for several reasons: He broke up the large railroad corporations. He made America a more active voice in world politics. He won the first Nobel Peace Prize given to an American, for his help in ending the war between Russia and Japan. (In dealing with other nations he followed the slogan "Speak softly and carry a big stick.")[6]

Woodrow Wilson followed William H. Taft as President. He guided the nation through World War I, and won passage of legislation that helped him use his authority. President Wilson held the first regularly scheduled press conferences. He was also the first President since John Adams to address a joint session of Congress concerning the State of the Union. After the war, Wilson worked to form a League of Nations. For political reasons, the Treaty of Versailles, which contained a provision for setting up the League of Nations, was defeated in the Senate.

Franklin D. Roosevelt advanced the presidency by continuing Theodore Roosevelt's and Woodrow Wilson's practice of active involvement in the legislative process. FDR took office in 1933, in the midst of the Great Depression. America entered World War II during his term. He revived the press conference, which had declined under Presidents Harding, Coolidge, and Hoover. He used his famous "fireside chats" over the radio to reach the American public.

Roosevelt also led Congress in developing many new federal programs and agencies. In the first one hundred days of his administration, Congress passed fifteen acts for his New Deal.[7] At President Roosevelt's urging, laws were passed to provide old age pensions, unemployment insurance, aid to dependent children, and health services. Franklin Roosevelt was elected to four consecutive terms, but died just three months after taking office in 1945.

Harry Truman became President upon the death of Franklin D. Roosevelt. President Truman knew history, and he greatly admired Presidents Thomas Jefferson, Andrew Jackson, and Woodrow Wilson. Truman was admired by others for his willingness to accept responsibility. (On his desk was a sign that read "The buck stops here.") When he left office after his second term, Truman was one of the nation's most respected Presidents.[8]

These are six Presidents who, according to Rossiter, also were important for "strengthening" the presidency:[9]

- John Adams, the second President, for his dignity and patriotism.

- James K. Polk, for promoting national unity and harmony.

- Andrew Johnson, for standing up to political opponents in Congress.

- Rutherford B. Hayes, for his determination in naming his cabinet, getting civil service reform, and dispatching troops in the railroad strike of 1877.

- Grover Cleveland, for his independence and honesty.

- Dwight D. Eisenhower, for keeping intact the power and prestige of the presidency, and for giving Americans a peaceful time after the end of World War II.

Presidents after Eisenhower have also made unique contributions to the office. John F. Kennedy used his power as President to launch new civil rights legislation at home. He also sent Americans abroad with the Peace Corps to help developing countries. Richard Nixon made Americans aware of the dangers of an imperial presidency. Ronald Reagan reenforced the President's power as commander in chief, when he sent the military to invade Grenada in 1983, and sent troops to help with a peacekeeping force in Beirut, Lebanon. George Bush reestablished the presidency as a major force in setting and carrying out U.S. foreign policy.

The list could be much longer, since each President has often been studied and rated, according to strengths and weaknesses. Many books have been written about each President's contributions.

▶ Reflections on the Presidency

Some Presidents were happy to leave office. Martin Van Buren once remarked, "As to the presidency, the two happiest days of my life were those of my entrance upon the office and my surrender of it."[10] John Quincy Adams recalled his years as President as "the four most miserable" of his life.[11] Jefferson described the presidency as "a splendid misery," and Jackson saw it as "dignified slavery."[12]

Others have left office with regret. The energetic and enthusiastic Theodore Roosevelt said upon leaving office, "No president has ever enjoyed himself as much as I have enjoyed myself, and for the matter of that I do not know of any man of my age who has had as good a time."[13] Ronald Reagan said that he enjoyed every aspect of the presidency. "Even after eight years, the experience of walking into a crowded House of Representatives to deliver a speech sent a chill down my spine."[14] In his speeches, George Bush often said, "In case you hadn't noticed, I really love my job."[15]

Regardless of his feelings upon leaving the office, each President has added his own unique chapter to the story of the presidency.

Historian Bruce Catton once wrote of the presidency:

> If the story of the Presidents proves nothing else, it testifies to the enormous stability of the office itself and of the Nation that devised it. . . . Every man who ever lived in the White House understood that he was acting for something much bigger than himself. . . . Only a Nation with sound instincts for the survival of freedom, democracy and the national well-being could have chosen a group that stands the backward glance as well as this one does.[16]

George Washington set the standard over two hundred years ago. Each President who followed has tried to fill the office wisely and well.

Appendix:
Presidents and
Vice Presidents of the
United States

▶ Presidents

	Term in Office	Birth/Death
1. George Washington Wife: Martha	1789–1797	1732–1799
2. John Adams Wife: Abigail	1797–1801	1735–1826
3. Thomas Jefferson Wife: Martha	1801–1809	1743–1826
4. James Madison Wife: Dorothea (Dolley)	1809–1817	1751–1836
5. James Monroe Wife: Elizabeth	1817–1825	1758–1831
6. John Quincy Adams Wife: Louisa	1825–1829	1767–1848
7. Andrew Jackson Wife: Rachel	1829–1837	1767–1845
8. Martin Van Buren Wife: Hannah	1837–1841	1782–1862
9. William Henry Harrison* Wife: Anna	1841	1773–1841

The Presidency of the United States

	Term in Office	Birth/Death
10. John Tyler 1st wife: Letitia 2nd wife: Julia	1841–1845	1790–1862
11. James K. Polk Wife: Sarah	1845–1849	1795–1849
12. Zachary Taylor* Wife: Margaret	1849–1850	1784–1850
13. Millard Fillmore Wife: Abigail	1850–1853	1800–1874
14. Franklin Pierce Wife: Jane	1853–1857	1804–1869
15. James Buchanan	1857–1861	1791–1868
16. Abraham Lincoln* Wife: Mary Todd	1861–1865	1809–1865
17. Andrew Johnson Wife: Eliza	1865–1869	1808–1875
18. Ulysses S. Grant Wife: Julia	1869–1877	1822–1885
19. Rutherford B. Hayes Wife: Lucy	1877–1881	1822–1893
20. James A. Garfield* Wife: Lucretia	1881	1831–1881
21. Chester A. Arthur Wife: Ellen	1881–1885	1829–1886
22. Grover Cleveland Wife: Frances	1885–1889	1837–1908
23. Benjamin Harrison Wife: Caroline	1889–1893	1833–1901
24. Grover Cleveland Wife: Frances	1893–1897	1837–1908

	Term in Office	Birth/Death
25. William McKinley* Wife: Ida	1897–1901	1843–1901
26. Theodore Roosevelt Wife: Edith	1901–1909	1858–1919
27. William Howard Taft Wife: Helen	1909–1913	1857–1930
28. Woodrow Wilson 1st wife: Ellen 2nd wife: Edith	1913–1921	1856–1924
29. Warren G. Harding* Wife: Florence	1921–1923	1865–1923
30. Calvin Coolidge Wife: Grace	1923–1929	1872–1933
31. Herbert Hoover Wife: Lou	1929–1933	1874–1964
32. Franklin D. Roosevelt* Wife: Eleanor	1933–1945	1882–1945
33. Harry S. Truman Wife: Elizabeth (Bess)	1945–1953	1884–1972
34. Dwight D. Eisenhower Wife: Mamie	1953–1961	1890–1969
35. John F. Kennedy* Wife: Jacqueline	1961–1963	1917–1963
36. Lyndon B. Johnson Wife: Claudia (Lady Bird)	1963–1969	1908–1973
37. Richard M. Nixon** Wife: Patricia	1969–1974	1913–1994
38. Gerald R. Ford Wife: Elizabeth (Betty)	1974–1977	1913–
39. James Earl Carter Wife: Rosalynn	1977–1981	1924–

	Term in Office	Birth/Death
40. Ronald Reagan Wife: Nancy	1981–1989	1911–
41. George Bush Wife: Barbara	1989–1993	1924–
42. William J. Clinton Wife: Hillary Rodham	1993–	1946–

▶ Vice Presidents

	Term	Administration
1. John Adams	1789–1797	George Washington
2. Thomas Jefferson	1797–1801	John Adams
3. Aaron Burr	1801–1805	Thomas Jefferson
4. George Clinton	1805–1809	Thomas Jefferson
George Clinton*	1809–1812	James Madison
5. Elbridge Gerry*	1813–1814	James Madison
6. Daniel Tompkins	1817–1825	James Monroe
7. John C. Calhoun	1825–1829	John Quincy Adams
John C. Calhoun**	1829–1832	Andrew Jackson
8. Martin Van Buren	1833–1837	Andrew Jackson
9. Richard M. Johnson	1837–1841	Martin Van Buren
10. John Tyler	1841	William Henry Harrison*
(none)	1841–1845	John Tyler
11. George M. Dallas	1845–1849	James K. Polk
12. Millard Fillmore	1849–1850	Zachary Taylor*

	Term	Administration
(none)	1850–1853	Millard Fillmore
13. William King*	1853	Franklin Pierce
14. John C. Breckinridge	1857–1861	James Buchanan
15. Hannibal Hamlin	1861–1865	Abraham Lincoln
16. Andrew Johnson	1865	Abraham Lincoln*
(none)	1865–1869	Andrew Johnson
17. Schuyler Colfax	1869–1873	Ulysses S. Grant
18. Henry Wilson*	1873–1875	Ulysses S. Grant
19. William A. Wheeler	1877–1881	Rutherford B. Hayes
20. Chester A. Arthur	1881	James A. Garfield*
(none)	1881–1885	Chester A. Arthur
21. Thomas A. Hendricks*	1885	Grover Cleveland
(none)	1886–1889	Grover Cleveland
22. Levi P. Morton	1889–1893	Benjamin Harrison
23. Adlai E. Stevenson	1893–1897	Grover Cleveland
24. Garret A. Hobart*	1897–1899	William McKinley
25. Theodore Roosevelt	1901	William McKinley*
(none)	1901–1905	Theodore Roosevelt
26. Charles W. Fairbanks	1905–1909	Theodore Roosevelt
27. James S. Sherman*	1909–1912	William H. Taft
28. Thomas R. Marshall	1913–1921	Woodrow Wilson

	Term	Administration
29. Calvin Coolidge	1921–1923	Warren G. Harding*
30. Charles G. Dawes	1925–1929	Calvin Coolidge
31. Charles Curtis	1929–1933	Herbert Hoover
32. John N. Garner	1933–1941	Franklin D. Roosevelt
33. Henry A. Wallace	1941–1945	Franklin D. Roosevelt
34. Harry Truman	1945	Franklin D. Roosevelt*
(none)	1945–1949	Harry Truman
35. Alben W. Barkley	1949–1953	Harry Truman
36. Richard M. Nixon	1953–1961	Dwight D. Eisenhower
37. Lyndon B. Johnson	1961–1963	John F. Kennedy*
(none)	1963–1965	Lyndon B. Johnson
38. Hubert H. Humphrey	1965–1969	Lyndon B. Johnson
39. Spiro T. Agnew**	1969–1973	Richard M. Nixon
40. Gerald R. Ford	1973–1974	Richard M. Nixon**
41. Nelson A. Rockefeller	1974–1977	Gerald R. Ford
42. Walter F. Mondale	1977–1981	James Earl Carter
43. George Bush	1981–1989	Ronald Reagan
44. Dan Quayle	1989–1993	George Bush
45. Albert Gore, Jr.	1993–	William J. Clinton

* Died in office/ ** Resigned

Glossary

American Revolution—The war for American independence from Great Britain (1775–1781).

Articles of Confederation—An agreement among the thirteen original Colonies, approved in 1781, that provided a loose federal government, prior to the Constitution.

cabinet—The body of advisors to a head of state.

capitol—The building in which a legislative body meets.

checks and balances—Constitutional provisions that provide for a balance of power among the three branches of government.

Chief of Staff—The President's personal advisor, and head of the White House Office.

Colonies—The collective term for the thirteen original American colonies; a term used before they became states officially.

Constitution—The fundamental law of the United States, put into effect in 1789; replaced the Articles of Confederation.

Continental Congress—An assembly of delegates from the thirteen original Colonies; governed during the American Revolution.

Declaration of Independence—Document establishing the United States as a nation independent from Great Britain.

executive branch—Branch of U.S. government responsible for enforcing the law; headed by the President and Vice President.

elector—One qualified to vote in an election; one who is a member of the U.S. electoral college.

electoral college—The electors who meet, after citizens vote for President, to cast ballots for the President and Vice President.

Executive Office of the President—A collection of agencies, directly responsible to the President, that help the President administer the executive branch of the government.

executive order—An order issued by the President that becomes law without prior approval by Congress.

executive privilege—A principle whereby the President may prevent Congress and the courts from questioning executive officials without his express consent.

formal power—Presidential power that originates in the Constitution, in laws passed by Congress, and in judicial interpretations.

inherent power—Presidential power that comes from on-the-job interpretation, rather than from constitutional or statutory law.

judicial—Relating to the courts, or to the judicial branch of government.

Oath of Office—The promise made by a U.S. President upon taking office.

Oval Office—The President's office, located in the West Wing of the White House.

pardon—An order that erases both sentence and guilt, as if a crime had never been committed.

pocket veto—The nonpassage of a bill that occurs if the bill does not become law because Congress adjourns before the ten-day time limit for presidential vetoes passes, and the President does nothing.

Glossary

Shays' Rebellion—An uprising of farmers led by Daniel Shays in 1787 to protest Massachusetts' refusal to issue paper money.

State of the Union—The President's annual address to Congress, required by the Constitution.

War Powers Resolution—Passed by Congress in 1973 as an attempt to check the President's power to commit troops to fight.

White House—The official residence for the President of the United States. Located at 1600 Pennsylvania Avenue, Washington, D.C.

Whiskey Rebellion—Riot by Pennsylvania farmers in 1794, over their refusal to pay federal taxes on whiskey.

Chapter Notes

Chapter I

1. Richard Norton Smith, *Patriarch—George Washington and the New American Nation* (New York: Houghton Mifflin Co., 1993), p. 21.

2. Ibid., pp. 23–24.

3. Paul F. Boller, Jr., *Presidential Anecdotes* (New York: Oxford University Press, 1981), p. 120.

4. Congressional Quarterly, *Cabinets and Counselors—The President and the Executive Branch* (Washington, D.C.: Congressional Quarterly, Inc., 1989), pp. 113, 141.

5. Michael Nelson, ed. *Congressional Quarterly's Guide to the Presidency* (Washington, D.C.: Congressional Quarterly, Inc., 1989), p. 805.

6. U.S. Dept. of Commerce, Economical and Statistical Administration, Bureau of the Census, *Statistical Abstract of the United States—The National Data Book*, 1993, p. 343.

Chapter 2

1. Eleanor Goldstein and Joseph Newman, ed., *What Citizens Need to Know About Government* (Washington, D.C.: U.S. News & World Report Books, 1983), p. 4.

2. *The 1994 Information Please Almanac Atlas and Yearbook*, 47th ed. (Boston & New York: Houghton Mifflin Company, 1994), p. 614.

3. Congressional Quarterly, *Powers of the Presidency* (Washington, D.C.: Congressional Quarterly, Inc., 1989), p. 1.

4. David C. Whitney, *The American Presidents—Biographies of the Chief Executives From Washington Through Bush* (New York: Prentice Hall Press, 1990), p. 27.

5. Frank Freidel, *The Presidents of the United States of America* (Washington, D.C.: White House Historical Association, 1989), p. 57.

∨∨∨∨∨∨∨∨∨∨∨∨∨∨∨∨∨∨∨∨∨∨∨∨∨∨∨∨∨

6. Roy F. Nichols, *The Invention of the American Political Parties—A Study of Political Improvisation* (New York: Macmillan Co., 1967), p. 390.

7. Alex Wellek, ed., *The Encyclopedic Dictionary of American Government* (Guilford, Conn: The Dushkin Publishing Group, Inc., 1991), pp. 314, 315.

8. Barbara Silberdick Feinberg, *American Political Scandals, Past and Present* (New York: Franklin Watts, 1992), p. 116.

9. Whitney, p. 365.

10. Ibid.

Chapter 3

1. Clifton Fadiman, ed., *The Little, Brown Book of Anecdotes* (Boston: Little, Brown and Co., 1985), p. 328.

2. Clinton Rossiter, *The American Presidency* (New York: Harcourt, Brace & World, Inc., 1960), pp. 15–43.

3. Congressional Quarterly, *Powers of the Presidency* (Washington, D.C.: Congressional Quarterly, Inc., 1989), p. 24.

4. Donald L. Robinson, *"To the Best of My Ability"—The Presidency and the Constitution* (New York: W.W. Norton & Co., 1987), p. 112.

5. Judie Mills, *John F. Kennedy* (New York: Franklin Watts, 1988), p. 226.

6. Congressional Quarterly, p. 86.

7. Ibid., p. 95.

8. Ibid., p. 172.

9. Rossiter, p. 99.

10. Ibid., p. 105.

11. Congressional Quarterly, p. 98.

12. Ibid., p. 71.

13. Ibid., p. 59.

14. David C. Whitney, *American Presidents—Biographies of the Chief Executives From Washington Through Bush* (New York: Prentice Hall Press, 1990), p. 37.

∧∧∧∧∧∧∧∧∧∧∧∧∧∧∧∧∧∧∧∧∧∧∧∧∧∧∧∧∧

15. *The 1994 Information Please Almanac* (Boston: Houghton Mifflin Co., 1994), p. 385.

16. Michael Kronenwetter, *The Military Power of the President* (New York: Franklin Watts, 1988), pp. 119, 120.

17. Jimmy Carter, *Keeping Faith—Memoirs of a President* (New York: Bantam Books, 1982), p. 27.

18. Rossiter, pp. 34–35.

19. Samuel L. Popkin, *The Reasoning Voter— Communication and Persuasion in Presidential Campaigns* (Chicago: University of Chicago Press), 1991, p. 28.

20. Congressional Quarterly, pp. 245–246.

Chapter 4

1. Lonnelle Aikman, *The Living White House* (Washington, D.C.: White House Historical Association, 1991), p. 137.

2. Judith St. George, *The White House—Cornerstone of a Nation* (New York: G.P. Putnam's Sons, 1990), p. 92.

3. Aikman, p. 27.

4. David McCullough, *Truman* (New York: Simon & Schuster, 1992), pp. 397–398.

5. "The White House," undated fact sheet received from the White House Liaison, p. 6.

6. St. George, pp. 124, 132–133.

7. "The White House," p. 7.

8. Christopher Georges, "Executive Sweet," *The Washington Monthly*, January–February 1993, p. 35.

9. J. B. West, *Upstairs at the White House—My Life With The First Ladies* (New York: Coward, McCann & Geoghegan, Inc., 1973), p. 137.

10. Michael Duffy and Dan Goodgame, *Marching in Place—The Status Quo Presidency of George Bush* (New York: Simon & Schuster, 1992), p. 39.

11. Bart Handford, Office of Presidential Scheduling, The White House, Washington, D.C., "Schedule of the President for Wednesday, February 2, 1994."

12. Margaret Brown Klapthor, *The First Ladies* (Washington, D.C.: White House Historical Association, 1989), p. 73.

13. Ibid., p. 79.

14. Rosalynn Carter, *First Lady From Plains* (Boston: Houghton Mifflin Co., 1984), pp. 183–184.

15. Fred Bruning, "A Question of Credibility," *Maclean's*, March 28, 1994, p. 9.

16. Ronald Kessler, *Inside The White House* (New York: Pocket Books, 1995), p. 23.

17. *Facts on File: Weekly World News Digest with Cumulative Index* (New York: Facts on File, 1993), p. 518.

18. Kessler, p. 157.

19. Michael Nelson, ed. *Congressional Quarterly's Guide to the Presidency* (Washington, D.C.: Congressional Quarterly, Inc., 1989), pp. 839–840.

20. William Seale, *The President's House—A History* (Washington, D.C.: White House Historical Association, 1986), p. 264.

21. Jimmy Carter, *Keeping Faith—Memoirs of a President* (New York: Bantam Books, 1982), pp. 29–30.

22. McCullough, pp. 808–811.

23. Gerald Ford, *A Time To Heal—The Autobiography of Gerald Ford* (New York: Harper & Row Publishers, 1979), pp. 309–312.

24. Ronald Reagan, *An American Life* (New York: Simon & Schuster, 1990), pp. 259–263.

25. Melinda Liu and Douglas Waller, "Terror on the South Lawn," *Newsweek*, September 26, 1994, p. 42.

26. Laurie Asseo, "The Charge: Trying to Kill Clinton," *USA Today*, November 18, 1994, p. 4A.

27. George E. Reedy, *The Twilight of the Presidency—An Examination of Power and Isolation in the White House* (New York: World Publishing Co., 1970), p. 12.

28. Ibid., p. 194.

Chapter 5

1. Frank Freidel, *The Presidents of the United States of America* (Washington, D.C.: White House Historical Association, 1989), p. 11.

2. Michael Nelson, ed. *Congressional Quarterly's Guide to the Presidency* (Washington, D.C.: Congressional Quarterly, Inc., 1989), p. 841.

3. Michael Duffy and Dan Goodgame, *Marching in Place—The Status Quo Presidency of George Bush* (New York: Simon & Schuster, 1992), p. 40.

4. Congressional Quarterly, *Cabinets and Counselors—The President and the Executive Branch* (Washington, D.C.: Congressional Quarterly, Inc., 1989), p. 3.

5. Congressional Research Service, telephone conversation with author, November 22, 1994.

6. Jimmy Carter, *Keeping Faith—Memoirs of a President* (New York: Bantam Books, 1982), pp. 41, 42.

7. Duffy and Goodgame, p. 113.

8. Stephen E. Ambrose, *Eisenhower—The President* (New York: Simon & Schuster, 1984), p. 79.

9. Adam Nagourney, "One Year Later, President's Stars Still Shine," *USA Today*, January 31, 1994, p. 7A.

Chapter 6

1. Elizabeth Frost-Knappman, ed., *The World Almanac of Presidential Quotations* (New York: Pharos Books, 1988), p. 22.

2. Tom Wicker, *One of Us—Richard Nixon and the American Dream* (New York: Random House, 1991), pp. 533–534.

3. Congressional Quarterly, *Cabinets and Counselors—The President and the Executive Branch* (Washington, D.C.: Congressional Quarterly, Inc., 1989), p. 141.

4. Ibid., p. 145.

5. Joseph A. Califano, Jr., *The Triumph & Tragedy of Lyndon Johnson—The White House Years* (New York: Simon & Schuster, 1991), pp. 136–137.

6. Congressional Quarterly, *Cabinets and Counselors*, p. 151.

Chapter 7

1. Clinton Rossiter, *The American Presidency* (New York: Harcourt, Brace & World, Inc., 1970), p. 82.

2. Donald L. Robinson, *"To the Best of My Ability"—The Presidency and the Constitution* (New York: W.W. Norton & Co., 1987).

3. Rossiter, p. 89.

4. Frank Freidel, *The Presidents of the United States of America* (Washington, D.C.: White House Historical Association, 1989), p. 5.

5. David C. Whitney, *The American Presidents— Biographies of the Chief Executives from Washington Through Bush* (New York: Prentice Hall Press, 1990), pp. 73–74.

6. Ibid., p. 205.

7. Arthur M. Schlesinger, Jr., *The Coming of the New Deal* (Boston: Houghton Mifflin Co., 1959), p. 20.

8. Margaret Truman, ed., *Where the Buck Stops—The Personal and Private Writings of Harry S. Truman* (New York: Warner Books, 1989), p. 15.

9. Rossiter, pp. 106, 161.

10. Paul F. Boller, Jr., *Presidential Anecdotes* (New York: Oxford University Press, 1981), p. 199.

11. Lonnelle Aikman, *The Living White House* (Washington, D.C.: White House Historical Association, 1991), p. 26–27.

12. Ibid., p. 27.

13. Whitney, p. 205.

14. Ronald Reagan, *An American Life* (New York: Simon & Schuster, 1990), p. 387.

15. Michael Duffy and Dan Goodgame, *Marching in Place—The Status Quo Presidency of George Bush* (New York: Simon & Schuster, 1992), p. 49.

16. "The White House," undated fact sheet received from the White House Liaison, p. 5.

Further Reading

Aikman, Lonelle. *The Living White House.* Washington, D.C.: White House Historical Association, 1991.

Burford, Betty. *Al Gore: United States Vice President.* Springfield, N.J.: Enslow Publishers, Inc., 1994.

Cole, Michael D. *Bill Clinton: United States President.* Springfield, N.J.: Enslow Publishers, Inc., 1994.

Healy, Diana Dixon. *America's First Ladies: Private Lives of the Presidential Wives.* New York: Atheneum, 1988.

Paletta, Lu Ann, and Fred L. Worth. *The World Almanac of Presidential Facts.* New York: Pharos Books, 1988.

Seale, William. *The President's House.* Washington, D.C.: White House Historical Association, 1986.

St. George, Judith. *The White House: Cornerstone of a Nation.* New York: G.P. Putnam's Sons, 1990.

Whitney, David C. *The American Presidents: Biographies of the Chief Executives From Washington Through Bush.* New York: Prentice Hall, 1990.

Index